GLOBAL CITIZENSHIP

A PATH TO BUILDING IDENTITY

AND COMMUNITY IN A GLOBALIZED WORLD

Ron Israel

D1405154

ABOUT THE AUTHOR

Ron Israel has spent the past twenty-five years working in the field of international development. He has designed, managed, and evaluated large-scale development projects in education, public health, the environment, youth and workforce development, governance and citizen engagement. He has worked and consulted for Unicef, UNESCO, USAID, the World Bank, the World Food Programme, and numerous International Non-Governmental Organizations. Ron's experience, working in more than thirty countries in every region of the globe, brought him to the realization that building world community is one of the most important challenges facing our planet. He says that *"For me building a world community, composed of engaged citizens sharing a common set of values is the key to our sustainable future. It's what has led me to write my book."*

Ron did his undergraduate work at the School of Foreign Service at Georgetown University. He also holds a Master's Degree in International Public Administration from the Maxwell School at Syracuse University and a Master's degree in Social Science from the Center for West African Studies, University of Birmingham, UK.

Contents

INTRODUCTION

A global dimension has been added to the lives of most people on the planet. This new dimension gets manifested in many different ways, for example through the internet, the increased relationships we have with colleagues in other countries, the globalization of our economy, or our heightened concern about humanitarian crises and terrorism in different parts of the world. There are benefits and difficulties associated with the ways in which life is becoming globalized. However, like it or not, this new global dimension in our lives is here to stay, and quite likely will grow larger.

Our new global identity should force us to think and act differently about the ways in which we view the world. It should raise questions about how we relate to people from other countries, cause us to re-examine our perspective on world issues, and make us think more about the idea of belonging to a world community. But we need a metaphor and a framework that will enable us to constructively engage in these new ways. This book asserts that the most positive reaction to the globalization of our lives is to identify with the concept of global citizenship.

It is the goal of the book is to engage people in the process of learning more about what being a *global citizen* means. Most people have some awareness of the term and might even say, "Well sure, you can count me in; I see myself as relating to the idea." To which one might respond, "Great good first step. But what does the term *global citizen* really mean to you, and how are you incorporating it into your life?" It is at that point in the conversation that many people draw a blank, or say, "Well, I really care a lot about global warming or the earthquake and tsunami in Japan." But then can't go much beyond that.

So the book is intended to help readers look deeper into what it means to think of ourselves as *global citizens.* How seriously should we take this identity? What are its implications? Do we have to give up the citizenship we already have in our countries, our allegiances to race and cultural identity? What are our global citizenship values and responsibilities? What are the ways in which we can express ourselves in this new role? And why is the cultivation of global citizenship such an important activity in today's world?

The book is divided into four parts and sixteen chapters:

- **Part I** --The Emergence of The Global Citizen-- provides an introduction to the nature of modern day global citizenship; how it came about; and its implications for the ways in which we live. Chapter 1—*An Enabling Environment*—describes the forces that are globalizing our lives and shaping us into a world community. Chapter 2—*What Being Global Means*—portrays the global dimensions of fourteen different occupations. Chapter 3 – *Values and Responsibilities*—sets forth a set of values and suggestions that can help us better understand and fulfill our political roles as global citizens. Chapter 4—*Non-Political Expressions* —describes alternative ways in which people can express the values of global citizenship, from performing humanitarian service to creating world art and music. Chapter 5—*Myths* -- corrects common mistaken assumptions about global citizenship, for example you can't be a citizen of your country and still be a global citizen, or that global citizenship is a cult. Chapter 6 –*Globalization and Global Citizenship*—

makes an important distinction between *global citizenship* and the term *globalization*, as it is frequently defined.

- **Part II --** A Global Perspective-- focuses on the role that global citizens can play in solving the growing number of urgent political, economic, and social issues that confront our planet. Chapter 7--*Global Decisions Needed*—describes these important issues, and suggests how a global perspective is needed to help resolve them. Chapter 8—*Taking Action*—illustrates different ways in which global citizens are trying to address these world-wide issues.

- **Part III --**Global Governance-- focuses on the role that global citizens can play to help build more responsive and effective global governance institutions. It also summarizes lessons learned from previous efforts to establish systems of global governance and citizenship. Chapter 9 –*Organizational Profiles*—offers descriptions of organizations in different domains that provide a global governance function, including the United Nations, global professional organizations, and international non-governmental organizations. Suggestions are made as to ways in which those on the path to global citizenship can help support these organizations and monitor their performance. Chapter 10--*The Governance of Global Governance*---makes a case for having global governance institutions become more accountable to the people whom they are intended to serve. Chapter 11—*What History Teaches Us*-- provides lessons learned from previous efforts to establish systems of global governance and global citizenship. Chapter 12 –*Reinventing History*—contains an interpretation of human history as seen from a global citizenship perspective.

- **Part IV --** Moving Forwards -- has suggestions for ways of strengthening the practice of global citizenship and building world community. Chapter 13--*Signposts Along the Path*-- identifies positive as well as negative trends that are likely to influence the spread of global citizenship. Chapter 14 –*Strategies to Get There* – offers big-picture and more personal lifestyle strategies that are needed to build global citizenship and world community. Chapter 15—*Education for Global Citizenship*—provides a framework for how educators can design instructional programs that enable students to learn about the importance of global citizenship. Chapter 16 ---*Conclusion and Call to Action* ----sums up the importance of pursuing the path of global citizenship, as well as the challenges involved in doing so. At the end of the chapter is a Call to Action for the formation of a Global Citizen Leadership Association.

Who you are may influence the way in which you read the book. Those who are just beginning to learn about the path of global citizenship may be especially interested in Part 1. Those who feel they already have embarked on this path, and want to learn more about their roles and responsibilities, will be interested in Parts I and II. Those who are interested in deepening their commitment and playing a leadership role in the emerging global citizenship community will want to read the entire book.

I have wanted to write this book for some time. My parents raised me to think of myself as someone who belonged to the world. I tried to put into practice the idea they planted in me by working on issues of international development for several decades. Over the course of the past twenty-five years I have worked on issues of human development in more than thirty-five countries. But always during this time I kept coming back to the question, "Well what does belonging to the world really mean? What does it look and feel like in daily life?

It seems, early on in a new millennium that we can answer these questions in a very meaningful way; that we urgently need to answer them given the state of uncertainty, conflict, and suffering going on in the world; and that we now have the technology and communications needed to stitch us together into a world community to which all people can belong, *if we want to go there.* This book is betting that there are lots of people, young and old, interested in making the journey.

PART 1: THE EMERGING GLOBAL CITIZEN

> *A global citizen is someone who identifies with being part of an emerging world community, and whose actions contribute to building this community's values and practices.*

Chapter 1. An Enabling Environment

This is a book about an age of global citizenship, where people view the whole world as their home; where they move freely around the globe, pursuing dreams, having families, and constructing careers; building a village for themselves that transcends national boundaries; caring about the well being of their planet and contributing in different ways to making it a better place to live.

Crazy you say? Too idealistic? Perhaps. But, the age of global citizenship is moving rapidly towards us, if it is not here already. It's a response to a sense of belonging to the planet held by increasing numbers of people of different ages, cultures, and backgrounds It's also an age spurred by the forces of technology, communications, and transportation that enable us to give expression on a global scale to the human need for community.

The twenty-first century could indeed turn out to an age of global citizenship, a truly great period in history, an ultimate testament to the human spirit and the genius of our species; or it could turn out to be a nightmare, an Orwellian environment, ruled by totalitarian forces, in which humans become subservient to the technology they created; or, perhaps even worse, a planet filled with social turmoil, conflict, and disasters as the gap grows between the rich and powerful and the poor and the earth's climate warms. This book is intended as a guide to those interested in pursuing a path towards global citizenship; pointing out landmarks and warning signs, establishing a vision but also conveying words of caution about what might happen if the vision fails to be realized.

The idea of global citizenship is not necessarily a new one. From the time of Alexander the Great, spurred by the desire for military conquest, economic wealth or religious zeal, humans have always tried to construct empires (and conscript citizens) on a global scale. What is new today is the bottom-up push that is the driving global citizenship. There is not some mighty king or spiritual ruler organizing an empire and making us all their citizens. Rather increasing numbers of people all across the world are living lives that have become globalized; and, as a result, part of their identity as a person has a global dimension to it.

You, who view this document, are part of this trend. Whether you realize it or not, and most probably you do, the ways in which you live (the food you eat, the clothes you wear, the work you do) all have a global connection . Perhaps you are a young person trying to make sense of this changing world, a professional whose colleagues and networks span the globe, or someone who wants to do something about the humanitarian crises that seem to be taking place with increasing frequency in different regions of our planet. This book is intended to help give voice to the interconnectedness with the rest of the world that we all feel today in many different ways.

A distinguishing feature of such interconnectedness is its immediacy. You don't need to travel 10,000 miles around the world to instantaneously understand that a band of tropical air originating over the Sahara will soon impact the quality of your day in Europe or North America. You can just turn on your television or open your computer or cell phone and see a very vivid global weather map and get the big picture.

You don't need to wait weeks to know if your brother in Australia, who lives where a large terrorist attack has taken place, is OK. You can call him or text message or Skype him instantaneously on his smart phone or laptop. And you don't need to wait for tomorrow's newspaper to read about the scores of the World Cup regional matches or even watch the games; the scores and the games themselves come streaming through your computer or cell phone, along with an opportunity to share your opinion about which players did well and which didn't. This power of the *global now*, the fact that everything is in real time, the immediacy of access that we have to everyone and every event, reinforces the sense that we are all part of a global community.

Our sense of belonging also is deepened by the increasing transparency of everything we say and do. It is becoming increasingly difficult for anyone, especially public figures, to lead private lives. The actions of a corrupt politician are brought to life by a whistle-blowing government worker and then broadcast worldwide via social media. The trials and tribulations of famous movie stars and athletes are known and commented upon by millions of people around the world almost as soon as they happen. The classified secrets of diplomats and soldiers are leaked to an Internet freedom website and broadcast to the entire planet. One might argue whether so much public exposure of what was formerly thought to be private is a good thing. However our new "transparency" helps break down the communications barriers and social distances between people and their leaders. It also makes us reflect and be more prudent about our own behavior, knowing a modest indiscretion can soon become big news in distant places where we don't even know anyone.

The global dimension of this new "transparency" is unprecedented. Suddenly, countries and cultures, that from an historical point of view were always considered to be difficult to penetrate, are losing their veil of secrecy. Also, as people across the planet weigh in on-line about the latest personal crisis affecting a well known person in country X, we can see that supposed value differences between cultures are not as great as imagined; and that there is a common core of moral behavior shared by people from all different backgrounds and residences.

Global Citizenship asserts that, because our lives have become globalized, we need to see ourselves as part of an evolving world community. Our first task is to come together and take stock of values that we have in common. Perhaps those values include a commitment to social justice and basic human rights, a respect for the diversity of cultures and lifestyles on our planet, a belief that the earth is our home and must be cared for as such, or a commitment to democratic, participatory governance at all levels. Our major challenge as global citizens is to give better definition and expression to our core values, and have them inform the way in which we live our lives.

We also need to develop better mechanisms for making wise decisions about how we live and work as a world community. Nation states still dominate the political landscape, especially with regard to political matters and the use of organized force. However, in many other areas of human endeavor---economics, social relations, communications, the organization of our professional lives---national sovereignty is becoming increasingly impotent. Regulations, agreements, and codes of conduct are springing up from all kinds of different sources to meet the growing need for global governance. As global citizens, what do we know about these mechanisms? By what standards should they be held accountable for their policies and programs?

This book provides a framework for reflecting on issues of global citizenship. How are we to take on our new roles as citizens of the planet? What are our core values? What information will we need to have in order to make informed decisions about the global political, economic, and social issues that we face? What tools do we need to build a caring and sustainable world community? Guidelines are provided, suggestions made, and at the end of the book there is a Call to Action to form a Global Citizen's Initiative. Such an initiative would be a focal point for furthering the ideas expressed in the book and building world community.

Chapter 2. WHAT BEING GLOBAL MEANS

Being global means having a part of your life dependent upon and tied to people, places, and events in other parts of the world. Such a global connection can occur on many levels; for example, in the way in which the work you do is dependent on products and services from other countries; in what kinds of music you like, where the clothes you wear or the food you eat come from; or the distant origins of the weather we have and the air we breathe. For some people being global is a function of necessity; a requirement for doing the kind of work that they do; for others it's a moral imperative, brought on by the empathy they feel for victims of disasters or civil strife. With information and communication technologies, modern day transportation and travel, and the growth of international trade, we are constructing an economic and social infrastructure that makes it almost impossible to not be a global person in the twenty-first century.

Here are fourteen examples, some obvious, some hopefully surprising, of how the lives of many different types of people across the planet are becoming *globalized*:

 # 1 Advertisers and Marketers: frequently advise their clients to "go global" to expand the reach of their brand and greatly increase their customer base beyond national borders. For example, a recent article in *Howtodothings.com*[1] provides the following guidelines for young entrepreneurs that want to grow their businesses: " create a company name that people can freely interpret without any national or cultural preconceptions; create a website and an e-commerce page so that customers anywhere can buy your items with only a few clicks of their

mouse; choose delivery options that allow your product to be quickly shipped to a destination in any part of the world; install communications apps, like video conferencing or instant messaging that allow you to communicate with your suppliers, partners, and customers in real time across the world; and update yourself on global trends, whether a new payment system or an update on your web tools, that enable you to stay fresh in the global market.

 # 2 Astronauts: As a result of their time spent in space, astronauts often develop a global perspective on the wholeness and interconnectivity of the planet; As the astronaut Donald Williams said , "*For those who have seen the Earth from space, and for the hundreds and perhaps thousands more who will, the experience most certainly changes your perspective; the things that we share in our world are far more valuable than those which divide us.*"[2]

 # 3 Sports Team Owners and Athletes: They are increasingly engaged in competition on a global level. They include new countries in the expansion of their leagues and teams; participate in world games and contests; or recruit athletes from other counties in order to strengthen their team's capabilities. Global sporting events like the Olympics and the World Cup soccer matches unite the world as spectators and fans. The final match of the 2006 FIFA world cup was watched by 608,000,000 people around the globe, and was recorded as having the largest audience rating of any athletic event in history. Athletes who have had the privilege of competing at a global level especially in the Olympics, often have their perspectives changed. As Piere de Coubertin, one of the founders of the modern day Olympics said: "*The Olympic spirit is not the property of one race, nor of one age...May the Olympic Torch pursue its way through ages, increasing friendly understanding among nations.*"[3]

#4 Central Bankers: They have gone global because they recognize that the currencies and economies of their own countries can be effectively protected without mechanisms that allow their peers around the world to share information and work together. A common goal that most central bankers have is to guard against financial abuses anywhere in the world that, if left unregulated can rapidly spread and disrupt the operations of global markets.

#5 Stock Brokers and Investment Analysts: The well informed stock broker and investor must now be concerned with the status of economies in countries around the world; in the worth of stocks in emerging markets; in the index prices of foreign stock exchanges. The size of the world stock market in 2008 was estimated at 36.6 trillion dollars. The total world derivatives market was estimated to be 791 trillion dollars, 11 times the value of the entire world economy. Electronic communication networks (ECNs) facilitate market trading around the world, 24 hours a day, seven days a week, 365 days a year.[4]

#6 Farmers: Small-scale farmers around the world have a variety of perspectives on what it means to be global. Farmers in industrialized countries worry about how they can be protected from what can be produced at a lower cost in developing countries; while farmers in the developing world, where agriculture often is a large part of their nation's economy, are concerned about how to gain greater access to heavily protected foreign markets. Sometimes free-trade agreements, which bring economic efficiencies for large-scale industrialized producers, hurt the small-scale farmer. This is an issue that will be further explored in later chapters of our book.

#7 Diners: If you love to eat, as the saying goes, "the world is now your oyster." Riding advances in transportation, packaging and storage, food grown in one part of the world gets transported for consumption in another, often on the same day in which it is harvested. Cod caught off Norway is shipped to China to be turned into filets, and then shipped back to Norway for sale. Argentine lemons fill supermarket shelves on the Citrus Coast of Spain, as local lemons rot on the ground. Half of Europe's peas are grown and packaged in Kenya.

Increasingly efficient global transport networks make it practical to bring food, before it spoils, from distant places where labor costs are lower to middle and upper income consumers in Europe, North America and parts of Asia.. The penetration of mega-markets in nations from China to Mexico with supply and distribution chains that gird the globe — like Wal-Mart, Carrefour and Tesco — has accelerated the trend). Recently environmentalists have flagged the large carbon footprint involved in moving such agricultural commodities around the world; and are encouraging greater consumption of locally grown produce. However, the global marketplace for food is unlikely to abate, given growing consumer demand for foods that cannot be produced locally.

#8 Drug Dealers: They go global when they construct networks with middlemen and dealers in other countries that enable them to transport their product from producer to user. Two of the most cited examples of drug dealer global networks are the Latin American-based cocaine trail and the heroin trail that begins in the Golden Triangle of Asia. The production of cocoa and opium begins with peasant farmers who are provided a price (by guerillas, militias, and other narco-traffikers) that is sufficiently attractive to enable them to resist growing other crops. Those who purchase the base commodities arrange to process them into their narcotic derivative, and then move them through transit countries (in Mexico, the Caribbean and West Africa) to their ultimate destinations in Europe and North America. The global dealings of drug dealers affect all sorts of people at different levels----bankers, soldiers, police officers, and politicians. For those involved in the drug trade, being global implies a lifestyle often filled with violence, corruption, and lawlessness.

#9 Drug Enforcement Agents: They make agreements with their counterparts around the world that enable them to share information about criminals and collaborate in law enforcement operations. A good example of the internationalization of drug enforcement efforts is INTERPOL, the world's largest international police organization. INTERPOL identifies new drug trafficking trends and criminal organizations operating at the international level, and assists all national and international law enforcement bodies concerned with countering illicit production, trafficking, and abuse of drugs. *For more on INTERPOL see Chapter 8 below).*

 # 10 Presidents of Countries: Country presidents are being forced to go global. Leading historians, such as Robert J Shapiro and David M Kennedy, make the point that President Obama and other world leaders are forced to contend with the "erosion of national self-sufficiency." For example, because we live in an increasingly integrated world with globalized markets, many American jobs depend on the economic policies of governments in Europe, Asia or Latin America. National security is no longer predicated solely on the ability to negotiate treaties with other countries, but also on the movements of Al Qaeda and other terrorist organizations. Matt Bai of the Boston Globe, cites the presidential biographer Robert Dallek as saying: "What will end up defining this era of the presidency is the diminished power, the diminished authority, the diminished capacity to shape events. It's the presidency in eclipse."

#11 Musicians: They frequently collaborate and form bands with musicians from other countries and cultures, and contribute to the growing genre of world music. According to

Wikipedia, the term "world music" is taken as a classification of music that combines Western popular music styles with genres of non-Western music that were previously described as *folk music* or *ethnic music*. Paul Simon was one of the first people to popularize world music when he produced records that integrated a contemporary American folk/pop sound with melodies and rhythms from South Africa and Brazil

#12 Terrorists and religious fundamentalists: Terrorists are more about being global than being global citizens. They operate in a global environment, and rely on the internet to attract youth from around the World to their cause. Their view of a global society would be one in which everyone is a true believer. The use of the Internet by terrorists has skyrocketed in the past nine years. The number of websites operated by terrorist organizations has increased from 12 in 1998 to more than 4,800 in 2006. Terrorists use the Internet for data mining, networking, recruitment and mobilization, the distribution of instructions and online manuals, planning and coordination, fundraising and attacking other terrorists. They draw information from government sites for attacks; communicate via e-mail; recruit sympathizers in chat rooms; raise funds using online questionnaires; and settle arguments through postings in their websites.[5]

#13 University Presidents: They are motivated to be global for several reasons. First, they have a need to find students who can pay the ever-escalating tuition fees that most colleges and universities now charge. Secondly, they need to respond to the demand from their students for an environment that provides them with a more globalized educational experience. This is the reasons foreign students enrollments at US universities and colleges have increased on the average of 10% a year for the past five years; or why New York University, over the next several years, has organized degree granting campuses in Abu Dhabi, China, London, and other countries around the world, providing students with opportunities to move from one location to another, and transfer credits, as they pursue their degrees.

#14 Students: There is a growing demand for global education from students around the world. The New York Times recently conducted a study that participation by American high school students in an International Baccalaureate degree program was catching up to the more traditional prestigious Advanced Placement programs. U.S. campuses also continue to expand their commitment to study abroad.[6] In 2007 the number of Americans students receiving credit for study abroad exceeded 205,000. In China the number of Chinese students who went to study abroad in 2008 reached 179,800. 90% of this total was self-financed.[7]

The British Council's Student Decision Making Survey which gathered information on international studies from 115,000 students in 200 countries. Over the last three and a half years, international students exhibit distinct patterns for where, why and how they select the foreign country at which they will study. Students head to Britain for quality, the United State for career improvement and Germany for low tuition. The report also notes that the student market for overseas study is becoming "more sophisticated" due to greater domestic investment in higher education and more countries offering courses taught in English in non-English speaking countries (to overcome linguistic disadvantage). The cost of studying overseas is not a primary determining factor in where many students may choose to study.[8]

As the examples above point out, almost everyone in the world is leading a life that at least in part has become globalized. The new technology, communications, and transportation infrastructure that humans have put in place are connecting even the most isolated peoples.

The very same forces that are globalizing everyone and everything are also helping to fray the traditional identities of ethnicity, culture, nationality and race that have historically bound people together. It becomes harder to have your sole identify be with your ethnic group when members of your family travel to foreign countries and live, work, and intermarry with others. It becomes more difficult to only see yourself exclusively as a Frenchman, an American, or an Indonesian when your co-workers, the people you spend the most time with, are all from other countries. And it becomes more difficult to say that your religion is the only way when you see those from other faiths practicing and living up to the same spiritual values to which you aspire.

This is not to say that traditional identities are not still very important to people, and continue to be the primary way in which we define ourselves. The point is that these traditional identities, in many cases have loosened their hold somewhat, as more and more of our lives become globalized.

 # 15 You: You may want to examine the ways in which your own life has become globalized. Do you fit into one of the profiles described above? Are you aware of where your food and clothing come from and the conditions under which they were produced? What does an examination of your family tree tell you about your relationships to different countries and cultures? You may want to take the survey, provided in Appendix A to help determine the ways in which your lifestyle points in the direction of global citizenship.

Chapter 3. VALUES AND RESPONSIBILITIES

Being global is a fact of life for more and more people living on our planet, In many instances being global is the first step on a path that can lead to global citizenship. However being global does not necessarily mean pursuing a path of global citizenship, as the examples in Chapter 2 indicate. The globalization of our lives is creating great benefits and opportunities, but also much chaos and tumult. Many people are both benefitting and being hit hard by the globalization of their lives.A major premise of this book is that becoming a global citizen is the most positive response that a person can make to living in today's globalized environment. It is the response that most likely will ensure our own well being and the well being and long-term sustainability of our planet.

We make such an assertion recognizing that in a globalized world everything is up for grabs. Terrorists, radical extremists, religious fundamentalists, sovereign states, rogue states, multi-national corporations, and others are vying for control of the world. The fact that tools for globalizing your life are now available to almost everyone, means that the world is crowded with people trying to impose their point of view on others. We are at a point in history where various forces and ideologies are competing, consciously or unconsciously, for control of our planet.

In the 21st century the globalization of our lives will become more and more pronounced. The path to global citizenship says let's view this in a positive light. Let's draw on the best political and social ideas and values of our forbearers, and put them to work in a way that humanizes our globalized lives. If you are on the path to global citizenship, see yourself as belonging to a world community; know the values of that community; and feel that you have some level of responsibility for the welfare of the planet and the well being of others around the globe.

The world of the global citizen is a pluralistic world. It celebrates the diversity of the earth's people and cultures. However it is not a relativist world. It recognizes that there are values that cut across religion and culture and help bind us together as a species. Global citizens seek to articulate such common values, and promote their adoption. Below is a suggested set of eleven core values of a world community. Please review and reflect upon them. Are they the values of a world community in which you would want to live? Would you change the ways in which they are framed? Are there values that you think should be added to this list? Would you delete any of those already listed?

---

11 Core Values of a World Community

#1 BASIC HUMAN RIGHTS

#2 RELIGIOUS PLURALISM

#3 GENDER EQUITY

#4 PARTICIPATORY GOVERNANCE

#5 PROTECTION OF THE EARTH'S ENVIRONMENT

#6 SUSTAINABLE WORLDWIDE ECONOMIC GROWTH

#7 POVERTY ALLEVIATION

#8 HUMANITARIAN ASSISTANCE

#9 ELIMINATION OF WEAPONS OF MASS DESTRUCTION

#10 CESSATION AND PREVENTION OF CONFLICTS BETWEEN COUNTRIES

#11 PRESERVATION OF CULTURAL DIVERSITY

The responsibilities of global citizenship derive from values such as these. At a minimum those on the path of global citizenship should be aware of such values and feel attuned to them. However, we also need a cohort of leaders who can play active political roles in the world; advocating for international policies and agreements that reflect these values; monitoring the ways in which such values are aligned with the policies and practices of global governance institutions; and educating others about the importance of such values to their lives and to the building of a sustainable, caring world community.

On a political level, global citizen leaders are needed to help develop solutions to the growing number of political, economic, environmental, and social issues that affect our planet, for example: protection of the earth's environment and the preservation of our natural resources; the prevention of terrorism and the spread of weapons of mass destruction; the need for making common rules to address the globalization of trade or promoting the adoption of behaviors that prevent worldwide health pandemics. Global citizen leaders need to better understand these issues, articulate how they can best be addressed from a global perspective, and then advocate for that perspective with policy-makers and other key stakeholders.

Chapter 4. NON-POLITICAL EXPRESSIONS

It is unrealistic to think that all of us on the path to global citizenship must be political activists. People who share common values often find different ways of expressing them; and so there are credible manifestations of global citizenship that focus on the "softer" side of what being a citizen means. Here are people interested in building caring relationships with those in other parts of the world -- providing humanitarian service, becoming global social entrepreneurs, building friendships with people in other countries, joining international professional associations, or creating world art and music. Chapter 4 provides some suggestions about how to become engaged in the non-political dimensions of global citizenship.

- **PROVIDING GLOBAL HUMANITARIAN SERVICE:**

A place to start is to engage with one of the many organizations that respond to the humanitarian needs of countries in crisis. For example, whether living in the United States, Cuba, Europe, or China, many hundreds of thousands of people felt a sense of connection to the situation in Haiti. In schools, religious centers, and family gatherings throughout the world, people talked about what happened in Haiti, why it happened, and what they could do to alleviate the suffering there. These conversations moved many people to think outside of their daily local interests and linked them to a global conversation about basic needs, human rights, and collective responsibilities.

The global humanitarian response to the Haitian earthquake is but one example of how people across the planet are responding to humanitarian crises in different parts of the world. The 2008 Asian tsunami, the recent record-breaking floods in Pakistan, the oil spill in the Gulf of Mexico, and the recent devastating earthquake and tsunami in Japan are further examples of how people living in places far removed from the scene of a natural disaster, or a man-made crisis, reach-out and speak-out to help their neighbors.

There are literally thousands of humanitarian service organizations that need your help. The world's largest humanitarian organization is the International Federation of Red Cross and Red Crescent Societies. The Federation coordinates the efforts of 186 national Red Cross and Red Crescent societies to provide international humanitarian assistance. These efforts support assist millions of the world's most vulnerable people; victims of natural and man-made disasters, refugees and displaced people and those hit by socio-economic problems. The Federation's work is guided by seven fundamental principles and humanitarian values ---- *humanity, impartiality, neutrality, independence, voluntary service, unity, and universality.*[9]

Crisis response is not the only way in which those interested in global humanitarian service can make a contribution. There are other opportunities such as sponsorship programs that provide support to families in need. All over the globe individuals enlist in sponsorship programs and support vulnerable children and families by contributing a small amount of funding on a consistent basis. This is not a new phenomenon, but originated as a response to the devastation felt in many European countries as a result of World War II. In 1945, Save the Children, an international Non-Governmental Organization (NGO) introduced a unique humanitarian sponsorship program. The program allowed for Canadian citizens to sponsor refugee children from Yugoslavia who were sheltered in Sweden during World War II for $96.00 per year.[10] This innovative program paved the way for a wide variety of global people-to-people sponsorship programs that Save the Children and other NGOs have developed over the years.[11] Here are some short examples:

- *Kiva*, an international micro-lending NGO, has utilized the power of people-to-people lending to help alleviate poverty. By supporting Kiva you can help empower individuals from varying communities to lend a small amount of money, through the Internet, to an entrepreneur living in a different part of the world. This small loan helps its beneficiaries. By enabling them to take a step out of poverty and provide economic support for themselves, their families, and communities.[12]

- *World Vision* is a Christian relief, development and advocacy organization dedicated to working with children, families and communities to overcome poverty and injustice. It organizes people-to-people child sponsorship programs in almost 100 countries As a sponsor, for $35.00 a month you can help provide a child with sustainable access to life-sustaining basic resources like nutritious food, clean water, healthcare, and education.[13]

- *The Heifer Project* works with communities to end hunger and poverty and care for the earth. It enables you to support livestock sponsorship programs that help families improve their nutrition and generate income in sustainable ways. Heifer sponsorship programs are referred to as "living loans" because in exchange for their livestock and training, families agree to give one of its animal's offspring to another family in need.[14]

- *Habitat for Humanity* seeks "to eliminate poverty housing and homelessness from the world and make decent shelter a matter of conscience and action. To accomplish these goals *Habitat* invites people of all backgrounds, races, and religions to build houses together in partnership with families in need. Since its founding in 1976, global citizens working on *Habitat* projects have built over 350,000 houses around the world, providing more than 1.75 million people with safe, decent, affordable shelter.[15]

The International Federation of Red Cross and Red Crescent Societies, Kiva, World Vision, the Heifer Project, and Habitat for Humanity are illustrative examples of humanitarian organizations that can use your help. For a directory of such organizations see www.devdir.org, ngodirectory.net or wango.org. Visit these and other websites and locate a global humanitarian service organization whose mission appeals to you.

- **BUILDING GLOBAL FRIENDSHIPS AND RELATIONSHIPS**

As the world becomes increasingly linked, we have greater opportunities to establish personal friendships and relationships with people in other parts of the world. For example, with the development of chat tools and cell phone applications, someone sitting in London is able to communicate with another person in Shanghai in an instantaneous manner that makes geographic distance irrelevant. With the development of social media such as Twitter and Facebook, people with access to the Internet are able to stay in constant contact and up to date on the lives of friends living in different time zones and regions of the world. Facebook, one of the most popular social networking websites to date, has over 500 million active users.[16]

Enhanced real-time and virtual mobility are leading to the loosening of tightly held racial, cultural, and ethnic identifies. In 2000, for the first time in U.S. Census history, Americans were given the opportunity to check more than one box when questioned of their race. That year, nearly 7 million people claimed to be multiracial. Though results of the 2010 have not been fully analyzed, Census officials believe that this number has grown by over 25% since the 2000 census.[17]

- **JOINING GLOBAL PROFESSIONAL ASSOCIATIONS**

International professional associations are another manifestation of the "soft side" of global citizenship. Many occupations have developed global professional associations that help members network with one another, exchange lessons learned, and establish regulations and standards to govern their field. If you are a member of a profession, or considering joining one, you may want to find out if there is an international professional association that you can join. Here are some examples:

- The *International Civil Aviation Organization (ICAO)* was established in order to standardize, regulate, and promote the development of international air transport. ICAO is made up of 189 member countries who are required to follow a multitude of ICAO developed standards, including but not limited to, air travel safety, border crossing procedures, takeoff and landing procedures, as well as rules regarding aircraft construction. As people continue to fly more frequently and in increased numbers, these regulations play a significant role in ensuring passenger safety.[18]

- *International Federation of Accountants (IFAC)* is a global governance organization for the accountancy profession. IFAC is an association whose members are national accounting associations from 164 countries. IFAC strives to serve the public interest through the development of international standards in auditing, education, ethics, and public sector financial reporting; by advocating transparency and convergence in financial reporting; by providing best practice guidance for professional accountants employed in business; and by implementing a membership compliance program. IFAC members are professional accountancy organizations recognized by law or general consensus within their countries as substantial national organizations.[19]

- *International Association of Fire Chiefs* represents the leadership of over 1.2 million firefighters and emergency responders. IAFC members are the world's leading experts in firefighting, emergency medical services, terrorism response, hazardous materials spills, natural disasters, search and rescue, and public safety legislation. Since 1873, the IAFC has provided a forum for its members to exchange ideas and learn about the latest products and services available to first responders.[20]

- *World Wide Web Consortium (W3C)* is the main international standards organization for the World Wide Web. The consortium is made up of leading World Wide Web technical organizations from around the world. It has full-time staff that work together in the development of standards for the World Wide Web. As of 18 January 2011, the World Wide Web Consortium (W3C) had 322 members. W3C also engages in education and outreach, develops software and serves as an open forum for discussion about the Web.

W3C was created to ensure compatibility and agreement among industry members in the adoption of new standards. Prior to its creation, incompatible versions of HTML were offered by different vendors, increasing the potential for inconsistency between web pages. The consortium was created to get vendors to agree on a set of core principles and components which would be supported by everyone.

W3C is jointly administered by the MIT Computer Science and Artificial Intelligence Laboratory (CSAIL, located in Stata Center) in the USA, the European Research Consortium for Informatics and Mathematics (ERCIM) (in Sophia Antipolis, France), and Keio University (in Japan). W3C also has World Offices in sixteen regions around the world. W3C Offices work with their regional Web communities to promote W3C technologies in local languages, broaden W3C's geographical base, and encourage international participation in W3C Activities.[21]

Global professional associations, like those described above, today cover a wide range of occupations that range from the International Organization of Robotics (IOR) to the International Association of Forensic Linguists (IAFL). This growing number of worldwide professional organizations is another reflection how quickly life and work is becoming globalized.

- **CREATING WORLD ART AND MUSIC**

The globalization of our lives also is having a large impact on the arts. It has facilitated the ability of artists and musicians from different countries and cultures to collaborate with one another and develop new global fusion art forms, for example:

- *The Global Art Project* sponsors an International Art Exchange for Peace. Participants display artwork, in any medium, that depicts their own vision of peace and goodwill.[22] Another project, "The One Million Masterpiece," Project, aims to bring together one million artists to create a compelling image of a global society. This project claims to be the largest collaborative art project in the world.[23]

- *Indaba Music:* In 2007, Indaba Music was launched in order to create a space for musicians, living in various parts of the world, to collaborate through the Internet (Indaba means "sharing" in Zulu). Indaba has over 500,000 members ranging from amateur musicians to Grammy Award winners. Through the utilization of the Internet, and Idaba's online tools, artists are able to come together and make music with one another. An American music critic said of Indaba: "These people can come together and make incredible creations. I'll give it up, they're wonderful."[24]

- *Playing for Change* is a multimedia movement whose mission is to inspire, connect, and bring peace to the world through music. The idea for this project arose from its founders' belief that music has the power to break down boundaries and overcome distances between people. Playing for Change's commitment is to organize an

environment for musicians where they can create freely and where there are no barriers

between them and those who would eventually experience their music. Playing for

Change musicians put on shows around the world. When audiences see and hear

musicians from different countries who have traveled thousands of miles from their

homes, united in purpose and chorus on one stage, everyone is touched by music's

unifying power.[25]

- PARTICIPATING IN GLOBAL ATHLETIC EVENTS

Participating in the Olympics and other global sporting events often represents the pinnacle of

an athlete's career. The 2008 Olympic games in Beijing brought together 11,028 athletes from

204 National Olympic Committees who competed in 28 sports for top positions in the world of

athletics.[26] Though participation in these games elicits national pride, it also helps build global

community among athletes by encouraging sportsmanship and interaction between

participants from different countries. The games also demonstrate how people from all over

share a common love for sports and support the ethics that govern open athletic competition.

Individual sports also are becoming globalized. For example, football (aka soccer in America) is

believed to be the most widely played sport in the world. In the 2010 World Cup football

tournament, over 200 countries competed for 32 spots.[27] In basketball, America's National

Basketball Association (NBA), perhaps the finest basketball league in the world, has many

foreign stars such as Yao Ming from China and Manu Ginobili from Argentina. Seventeen counties now have national basketball leagues and compete in the Olympics. Tennis and golf have long been established as global sports, with athletes from many different countries competing in tournaments throughout the world.

- **TRAVELING THE WORLD**

The sheer act of traveling to another country usually expands a person's horizons and makes us more aware of the greater world community. According to the U.N. World Tourism Organization, international tourism demand will double by 2020 to an astronomical 1.6 billion visitors generating nearly US $2 trillion in economic activity. Of this total 1.2 billion people will be intraregional tourists and 378 million will be long-haul travelers. The rise of low-cost airlines and cut-rate travel deals is fueling this projected upward trend in global demand. Today tourism represents 35 percent of the world's export of services and over 70 percent in many developing countries.[28]

The projected continuing growth of the tourism industry places great stress on natural habitats and indigenous cultures. Those on the path to global citizenship need to support tourism activities that have a low impact on the environment and local culture, while helping to generate income, employment, and the conservation of local ecosystems. These types of activities, known as sustainable tourism, seek to meet the needs of present day tourists and host communities while protecting and enhancing the needs of future tourists and the communities that will play host to them.[29]

- **IMMIGRATING TO ANOTHER COUNTRY**

Migration has the potential to increase economic interdependence and to reconcile the demographic challenges faced by older and younger countries. However migration also has the potential to act as a disruptive force, creating social and political tensions for many countries, and exacerbating crises caused by other factors, such as a sharp economic downturn. "Global migration affects all of us. We live in countries that are either places of origin, transit and/or destination for migrants. While the major countries of emigration are in the developing world, not all the major immigration countries are developed nations. In 2000 it is estimated that Western industrialized countries absorbed about 40% of the world's migrants."[30]

The world's immigrant population includes those who have chosen willingly to relocate their lives, those forced to migrate due to conflict and war, those who work abroad in order to send remittances back to their families, and gypsies who migrate as a way of life. A large number of immigrants do not migrate legally. In 2009 worldwide there were 20 to 30 million unauthorized migrants, 16 million people living in refugee camps, and nearly 26 million internally displaced persons (IDPs) in approximately 52 countries.[31] There are large refugee populations in many countries including: Afghanistan (1,300,000), Iran (1,300,000) Pakistan (1,200,000), the United States (485,000) and China (300,000)

Though many immigrants try to hold onto their traditional lifestyles, most inevitably adapt ways of living from customs found in their new countries. The UN Human Development Report estimates that there were nearly 214 million migrants internationally in 2010.[32] According to

33

the BBC, over the past 15 years, the number of people crossing borders in search of a better life has been rising steadily. At the start of the 21st century, one in every 35 people is an international migrant. If we all lived in the same place it would be the world's fifth largest country.

Many countries rely on migrant workers to provide important labor market functions. For example, in countries of the Arab Gulf, nearly 80% of workers are migrant workers coming from countries such as the Philippines, Indonesia, Sri Lanka, Nepal and Bangladesh. Immigrants also are an important part of the labor force in many of the world's industrialized countries.[33]

Money sent by migrants back to their countries of origin is an increasingly important source of outside funding for many developing countries. Remittance flows are the second-largest source, behind foreign investment by private companies, of external funding for developing countries.[34]

International cooperation on migration has generally been weak, and obstacles to greater cooperation are likely to remain considerable because of national sovereignty concerns. The absence of agreed upon international migration frameworks means there also are a lack of effective governance mechanisms to help countries work together to address immigration issues, including those related to humanitarian concerns. The risks to the world community of not trying to better manage migration are great.

Chapter 5. MYTHS

Some people, when they hear the term *global citizenship,* leap to the conclusion that this is a radical movement, which aims to establish world government, wipe out the nation state and any allegiances that people might have to their countries, cultures, and ethnicities. Chapter 5 was written to alleviate such anxieties, and calm the fears of those who think global citizens are just a bunch of crazy people.

Most of us today have multiple communities that call on our citizenship allegiance----our country, city or town, our ethnicity, the racial and religious groups to which we belong. These allegiances enrich our lives, and indeed enrich the path to global citizenship. In this context, it is important to take stock of what global citizenship means and what it doesn't mean. Such stocktaking enables us to better understand how to express our commitment to global citizenship's values and responsibilities, while not denying the other types of citizenships and allegiances that we all have. It also enables us to refute popular myths about who global citizens are and what they're seeking to achieve.

- **MYTH: YOU CAN'T BE A CITIZEN OF YOUR COUNTRY AND STILL BE A GLOBAL CITIZEN**

As global citizens, we accept the fact that multiple loyalties and allegiances—to family, religion, country, culture, and the planet at-large—are all a part of who we are. Global citizenship is part of a pluralistic, post-modern identity that many of us live with. It's an inclusive identity that embraces both the local and global, and rejects limited dichotomies of either/or and us and them. It involves a sense of ourselves that is grounded in specific places (home, local community), regions, and countries, but also includes having a sense of global belonging. Those on the path to global citizenship seek to build a world community that honors and respects such multiple allegiances.

Global citizenship does not in any way preclude someone from being patriotic and loving his or her country. On the contrary global citizenship depends also on having an identity, connection and understanding with a particular physical place on our planet. Our understanding of local issues, and the local environment in which we live is necessary information to share with those from other areas; as we learn about our differences while searching for the common ground that will help bind us together.

As global citizens, we also need to cast a critical eye when it comes to our country's policies vis-à-vis the rest of the world. For as much as we love our countries, we also are concerned about what is good and fair for the planet as a whole; and are not afraid to advocate for having our countries adapt a more global perspective in their foreign policies, when such a perspective is called for.

- **MYTH: GLOBAL CITIZENS ARE JUST A BUNCH OF RADICAL POLITICAL TYPES**

Both liberals and conservatives can stake claims to being global citizens. What matters most is the understanding we have, regardless of our political beliefs, that we are part of a world community, and share a commitment to expressing and building its values. We express its values by supporting basic human rights; working with others across the world to develop solutions to global problems; contributing to foreign humanitarian relief efforts, embracing

36

cultural diversity and religious pluralism; and advocating for accountability and transparency by the institutions responsible for global governance.

As global citizens we may have differences of opinion among ourselves. For example one person may view the need to emphasize the role of free markets that support world trade, while others may stress the need for global standards to address trade-related issues of economic equity and environmental impact. As global citizens, we need to develop mechanisms that facilitate dialogue discussion and consensus building among us. We also needs to be able to accept the fact that our members may share a commitment to common values and principles of global citizenship while differing on how best to solve global problems.

The world of the global citizen is a democratic participatory world, where differences of opinion are allowed to flourish; where debate and discussion among those from different cultures and points of view is encouraged; and where there is a commitment to developing fact-based, empirically tested solutions that work for the world as a whole, and not just a single country or interest-group.

- **Myth: Global citizens are members of a spiritual cult**

Religious pluralism is a core value of global citizenship. Global citizens believe in and respect the rights of others to practice their religion of choice. Any attempt at forced conversions or violent proselytizing goes against the grain of the kind of world we want to create. Any religious inspired war or global citizens should view act of terrorism as a misrepresentation of the true meaning of faith and spirituality.

Some people believe in new "earth religions" or planet spirituality, but these type of beliefs should not be equated with global citizenship either. They are just another form of religious expression that should be recognized and accepted along with other faiths.

Global citizens emphasize ecumenical dialogues between religious leaders. We have the conviction that at their core, all religions share certain common beliefs about morality and the nature of the human spirit. Certain spiritual precepts for example *love thy neighbor as thyself,* can be found in most major religions. These spiritual truths are manifested in various forms and transmitted through different religious teachings. The great spiritual teachers, regardless of their backgrounds and faith, are viewed as sharing a common understanding about principles of right and wrong and the human qualities needed to lead a good life.

- MYTH: GLOBAL CITIZENS ARE MEMBERS OF A HIGHLY EDUCATED GLOBAL ELITE

Global citizens come from all different backgrounds and walks of life. You can be an Eskimo in the Arctic, a Parisian housewife, Iranian student, Russian soldier, West African cocoa farmer, European philanthropist, American businessman or woman, or a Mongolian peasant. You can be almost anyone, anywhere, and be on the path to global citizenship (whether you know it or not). The point is that you shouldn't be able

Chapter 6. GLOBALIZATION AND GLOBAL CITIZENSHIP

The term *globalization*, as it is commonly used, is not the same thing as global citizenship, although some people confuse the two. Both globalization and global citizenship derive from the same wellspring of modern day technology, communications, and transportation systems. Globalization is the economic manifestation of this wellspring; global citizenship is the social manifestation. Global citizens need to understand the strengths and dangers of the phenomenon of globalization, and develop a perspective on how to relate to it.

Globalization is as an economic term that refers to the growing world-wide integration of the production of goods and services. Multinational or transnational corporations have generally been behind the movement towards globalization; making use of the forces of modern day technology communication and transportation to establish global production value chains that take advantage of regional differences in the costs of production. Prevailing economic wisdom about the virtue of free competition and open markets has been the ideological factor driving globalization. National and international policy makers, acting on this belief, have sought to aid globalization by promoting the reduction and removal of economic barriers between national borders in order to facilitate the flow of goods, capital, services and labor.

Thomas Friedman, in his landmark book, <u>The Earth is Flat,</u> argues that the pace of globalization picked up in the year 2000 as a result of the convergence of the personal computer with fiber-optic cable and the rise of work flow software. As a result " people all over the world started waking up and realizing that they had more power than ever to go global as individuals, they needed more than ever to think of themselves as individuals competing against other individuals all over the planet, and they had more opportunities to work with those other individuals, not just compete with them."[35]

Globalization has led to a vast increase in the magnitude of international trade, and in the relationship of trade to GDP. For example, according to David M Kennedy, Stanford University historian, for most of the 20th century foreign trade accounted for roughly 10 percent of America's G.D.P. That number started rising in the 1970s and now accounts for about 25 percent of G.D.P.

Globalization has both positives and negative attributes associated with it. Proponents make the case that it allows poor countries and their citizens to develop economically and raise their standards of living, while opponents to globalization claim that the creation of an unfettered international free market has benefitted multinational corporations at the expense of local enterprises, local cultures, and common people.

As this book asserts, global citizens may have different views on certain topics such as globalization. On the one hand a world where the free flow of goods, labor, and capital is facilitated supports a global citizen's ideal of freedom of economic exchange. On the other hand the disparities in labor and environmental standards between countries are cross-border equity issues that many global citizens feel need to be better addressed.

Another growing concern about globalization is that the integration of world economies may lead to the homogenization of life on the planet; that is wherever you go you will find the same Starbucks, Gap Store and McDonalds; and that this "malling" of the world also will result in the elimination of the world's cultural diversity. While the *homogenization of life hypothesis* is certainly a valid concern, it is by no means an inevitable. Human beings have been forever inventing and reinventing objects to buy and sell in the marketplace that seek to be better/different/more expensive or cheaper than what already exists. It is reasonable to think that human ingenuity will

PART II: A GLOBAL PERSPECTIVE

Chapter 7. GLOBAL DECISIONS NEEDED

There is another force that is driving the movement towards global citizenship: the need for urgent decision-making regarding the growing number of political, social, and economic issues that affect all of us. The list of world issues in need of some form of global governance seems to grow daily --- energy use and the environment; the management of scarce food and water resources; the control of weapon of mass destruction, world trade, drug prevention and others. Many of these issues place those of us on the path to global citizenship in a difficult position; what might appear to be a fair and equitable solution on a global perspective may not seem that way from a national or local viewpoint. Since all of us have multiple identifies, e.g. as citizens of our towns and countries as well as the world, we often have dilemmas of where to cast our allegiances.

The ways in which the people and countries of the world address, or fail to address, these issues reflect on the nature of global society and the character of global citizenship. In many instances what is needed is a better process for bringing together people and institutions from around the world and facilitating a discussion about similarities, differences and points of agreement in our viewpoints. There is an urgent need for those of us in the global citizenship community to construct forums where dialogue can take place on how to best make global solutions that benefit everyone.

In Chapter 7 we summarize several of the most important issues that confront the world community. We highlight the problems that each issue poses and then identify approaches to finding global solutions. The issues we discuss include our limited supply of natural resources and growing world population, mitigating climate change, economic growth and equity issues, preventing the spread of weapons of mass destruction, governance issues for failed states and countries in conflict, and the prevention and management of world health pandemics.

- **MAKING SENSIBLE USE OF OUR LIMITED SUPPLY OF NATURAL RESOURCES**

For those who live in the Western World, living standards are especially high. Citizens enjoy lucrative amenities – access to good food and clean water, cars, computers, televisions, and smart phones. We often are unaware where these resources come from, and assume they are in infinite supply. However, with the global population projected to rise to over 9 billion by 2050, and with more and more people wanting "Western-style" living standards, our current rate of natural resource use is unsustainable.

Global citizens need to become more aware of the issues affecting the use of the earth's natural resources, and contribute to efforts underway to promote sustainable resource usage. As a starting point, highlighted below are short summaries of the status of our supplies of oil, *fresh water, forests, agricultural products and fish.*

Oil: Oil is used to help support transportation, food production, manufacturing, construction, and scores of other daily activities. Our global demand for oil today is pegged at 80 million barrels a day and climbing. The oil industry does its best to meet this demand, but geologists estimate that world-wide production can be expected to decline by 2-3% a year for the foreseeable future. This projected decline is due to the slowly diminishing total amounts of oil that are readily available for extraction.[36] It is estimated that we have extracted 964 billion barrels of oil from known and accessible oil fields; and that there are another 764 billion barrels available from accessible fields and a further 142 billion barrels accessible from fields yet to be located. But at some point, which several scientists estimate to be 35-40 years from now, we will reach the limits of what can be readily extracted from our estimated 2 trillion barrel total supply of oil. Strategies to mitigate the current downward production trend include the use of new technologies such as horizontal drilling; improving the efficiency of our electrical grids; raising prices to encourage conservation; and making greater use of alternative energy sources, such as solar, wind, and biofuels.[37]

Fresh water: Only 2.59% of all water on earth is freshwater. Of this total 2% is trapped in ice caps and glaciers. The rest of our freshwater supply is in the form of groundwater, or is readily accessible water in lakes, streams, rivers, etc. It is estimated that 69% of worldwide water use is for agriculture, 22% is for industrial usage, and 8% is used to meet household needs.[38] The world's supply of clean fresh water is steadily decreasing as demand exceeds supply and the world population continues to rise. By the year 2025 scientists believe there will be large-scale water shortages among poorer countries, where resources are limited and population growth is rapid.[39]

Proposed solutions for preserving the world's supply of fresh water include: improvements in efficiency (e.g. irrigation systems often waste as much as 60% of the total water pumped before it reaches the intended crop); more efficient management systems; the use of technology, such as desalinization; and promoting conservation by removing water subsidies and letting prices be set in open markets.[40]

Forests: Forests cover 31 percent of the earth's total landmass of 4 billion hectares. The five most forest-rich countries (the Russian Federation, Brazil, Canada, the U.S. and China) account for more than half of our forest area. The UN Food and Agriculture Organization estimates that millions of hectares of forestland are destroyed each year (7.3 million hectares a year since 2000).[41]

Deforestation occurs for many reasons: trees are used for fuel or lumber, while cleared land is used as pasture for livestock, plantations, and settlements. The removal of trees without sufficient reforestation results in damage to habitat, biodiversity loss, and aridity.[42] Forests also act as carbon sinks, absorbing excessive CO_2 in the atmosphere. South America and Africa are the two regions of the world that are incurring the largest net loss of forest. Asia has recently moved from a net loss of around 800,000 hectares per year in the 1990s to a net gain of 1 million hectares per year this decade, an improvement linked to programs to restore forestlands.[43]

Agricultural Products: Each year, an ever larger portion of the world's basic agricultural crops, such as cassava and corn, sugar and palm oil, is being diverted for biofuels as developed countries pass laws mandating greater use of non-fossil fuels and as emerging powers like China and India seek new sources of energy. This "substitution effect" is having a major impact on world food prices. This year the U.N. Food and Agriculture Organization reported that its index of food prices was the highest in its more than 20 years of existence.

Soaring food prices have caused riots or contributed to political turmoil in many developing countries, such as Egypt and Bangladesh. The New York Times reports that experts are calling on countries to scale back their headlong rush into green fuel development, arguing that the combination of ambitious biofuel targets and mediocre harvests is contributing to high prices, hunger, and political instability.[44]

Fish: Fish account for roughly one fifth of all animal protein in the human diet, and around 1 billion people rely on fish as their primary protein source. Production of fish products is far greater than global production of poultry, beef, or pork. However a review of existing data by the World Resources Institute (WRI) indicates that " the contribution of fish to the global food supply is likely to decrease in the next two decades as demand for fish increases and production diminishes."

In 2006 an international group of ecologists and economists predicted that the world will run out of seafood by 2048 if steep declines of marine species continue at current rates. In 2003 – the last year for which data on global commercial fish catches is available-29 percent of all fish species had collapsed, meaning they are now at least 90 percent below their historic maximum catch levels.

Currently 80 million metric tons of fish are available each year for direct human consumption. This demand is expected to increase to 100 to 120 metric tons in the next several years as world population grows. Any shortfall in fish supplies is likely to affect developing nations more than developed nations. As demand and prices rise, exports of fish products from developing nations will tend to rise as well, leaving fewer fish for local consumption and putting fish protein increasingly out-of-reach for low income families. [45]

Substantial potential exists for increasing the ocean fish harvest with better management of fish stocks; eliminating harmful commercial fishing practices; reducing subsidies that governments provide to their fishing industries; and encouraging the growth of aquaculture.[46]

Global citizens need to develop a greater awareness about the status of natural resource uses, especially those in our own countries. We need to be aware of how the policies of our countries affect the use of our own natural resources, as well as those of other countries. And we need to adopt environmental friendly behaviors that help reduce our consumption of scarce natural resources, reduce our carbon footprint, and promote sustainable economic development. Examples of such behaviors include cutting down on the use of plastics, recycling of household waste products, installing more efficient home energy systems, and appliances, carpooling, and buying hybrids or cars that get good gasoline mileage.

Questions for global citizens to address: Who makes the decisions in our countries regarding the use and preservation of natural resources? What criteria are used to make these decisions? How has this criteria been developed? How should it be developed? Should we leave everything up to market forces? At what point should a natural resource be considered endangered? What can be done to address resource distribution issues, i.e. what if your country has an overabundant supply of certain resources while others don't have access to the supplies that they need?

- ### MITIGATING CLIMATE CHANGE

The issue of global climate change is an important issue to solve for its own sake, and because of the impact that global warming has on all the other global issues discussed in this book. The impact of global warming will be felt in terms of losses in economic productivity, more heat-related illness and disease; increased risk of drought, fires, and floods, rising seas, and habitat at-risk.

The amount of greenhouse gases in our atmosphere is proving that global climate change has become a significant issue threatening the well being of our planet. As a result of industrialization, population growth and the lack of environmental regulation, the amount of greenhouse gases increased dramatically by 26% from 1990 to 2005.[47]

Globally speaking, the first decade of the 21st century has been the warmest to date. In the last twenty years the intensity of tropical storms in the Atlantic Ocean, Caribbean and Gulf of

Mexico have increased dramatically. Six of the ten most vigorous hurricane seasons have transpired since the 1990's. Since 1870 sea levels have increased at a rate of approximately six-tenths of an inch per decade. Recently, this rate has increased to an inch per decade. This is believed to be an outcome of rising heat and the melting of Artic ice. In 2009, the amount of Arctic sea ice was 24% below the 1979 to 2000 average.[48]

The 3 billion people who live in poverty around the world will be hardest hit by climate change. The poor are more dependent on natural resources and have less of an ability to adapt to global warming's impact. Diseases, declining crop yields, and natural disasters are just a few of the impacts of climate change that could devastate the world's most vulnerable communities. The poorest also are those least responsible; as developing countries contribute only 10 percent of annual global carbon dioxide emissions.[49]

Strategies that the international community is pursuing to address global warming include: the establishment of international agreements, such as the Kyoto Protocol, to reduce greenhouse gas emissions; the establishment of emission standards, cap and trade systems, and other regulatory actions by individual countries or groups of countries; adaptation of sustainable environmental practices and the pursuit new green energy opportunities by the business community; and promoting the adoption of environmental-friendly lifestyle practices by individual citizens.

Global citizens can help advocate for these strategies and engage in the efforts of environmental organizations, such as the Nature Conservancy, World Wildlife Foundation, and Conservation

International that are working to address issues of climate change and global warming. We also can make changes in our personal lifestyles that lead to more environmentally friendly behavior, such as those described in the section above on the use of natural resources.[50]

Questions for global citizens to address: Should countries adapt tougher greenhouse gas standards? What has prevented them from doing so? How should we deal with the fact that countries differ in the manner in which they contribute to climate change? And how should we deal the differences in the impact of climate change between industrialized and developing countries? What are the international/global mechanisms that now exist for regulating climate change? To what extent have they been successful? How can they be improved?

- **ECONOMIC GROWTH AND EQUITY ISSUES**

World productivity has grown fivefold since 1950. Fueling this growth has been the steady integration of the global economy, characterized by increased international trade, the expansion of international financial markets, the spread of new technologies that have encouraged the development of transnational patters of production and consumption, and the large increase of foreign direct investment, especially in emerging economies. International trade now accounts for 25 percent of world GDP.[51]

A remarkable trend over the last 25 years has been the growth in the developing economies of east and south Asia. The largest economies in the world today now include China and India, as well as the United States, Japan, Germany, France, and the United Kingdom.[52]

Despite the upswing in world economic growth, some 100 countries in the developing world have experienced economic decline. In 70 of these countries average incomes today are lower than they were in 1980. Factors contributing to this decline include continued dependence on exports of primary commodities and falling commodity prices, trade barriers and restrictive currency exchange practices, high levels of indebtedness, slow progress with political and macroeconomic reform, and, in some countries, political instability and armed conflict. Poverty remains an enormous problem. About one third of the population of developing countries, 1.3 billion people, lives on less than US $1 dollar a day.[53]

The global financial crisis: Today changes in economic growth in developing and developed countries are closely interconnected due to the existence of the global economy. Such economic inter-dependence was made evident during the recent global financial crisis. The crisis began in 2007 and 2008 with the collapse of the US sub-prime housing mortgage market and the reversal of the housing boom in other industrialized countries. Around the world, stock markets fell, large financial institutions collapsed and governments had to come up with rescue packages to bail out their financial systems. Developing countries, many of whom lack the resources to counter such economic shock waves, were hard hit. For example it is estimated that economic growth in Africa was reduced by 2-4 percentage points as a result of the crisis.[54]

Jomo Kwame Sundaram, UN Assistant Secretary-General for Economic Development, reported that: "Large economies have taken fiscal stimulus measures, but poorer ones desperately in need of such steps—which are crucial for job creation—have not been able to do so.

International cooperation on the crisis has been inadequate. A much more coordinated economic recovery would have resulted in benefits for all major groups, especially the least developed countries.[55]

Global citizens need to develop increased awareness of how the actions of their country's financial institutions impact economic health and well being of people around the world. We need to identify ways in which global governance of the international financial sector can be strengthened to help prevent future crisis; and we need to advocate for international trading practices that ensure a level playing field for all countries, and mitigate the impact of export subsidies, tariffs, and currency manipulation.

> **Questions for global citizens to address**:   What steps can be taken to reduce the poverty gap between industrialized and developing countries? How did the recent worldwide financial crisis affect economic growth in different parts of the world? Has the international community done enough to respond to this crisis? If not, what more needs to be done?

- **PREVENTION OF THE SPREAD OF WEAPONS OF MASS DESTRUCTION**

Existing weapons of mass destruction (WMDs) act as a major threat to the global community. Their power of destruction is inextricably high. Wikipedia defines weapons of mass destruction as a "weapon that can kill and bring significant harm to a large number of humans (and other life forms) and/or cause great damage to man-made structures (e.g. buildings), natural structures (e.g. mountains), or the biosphere in general." Though the term WMDs often refers to nuclear weapons, biological and chemical weapons are included in this categorization as well.

Nuclear weapons Currently, eight countries have declared they possess nuclear weapons. They include China, France, India, Pakistan, Russia, the United Kingdom, the United States and North Korea. In addition, Israel and Iran are believed to have nuclear weapons, but have yet to declare them. On March 5, 1970, an international Nuclear Non-Proliferation Treaty, sponsored by the International Atomic Energy Agency (IAEA) came into effect in order to control the use and manifestation of nuclear weapons in the global community. This treaty commits states that do not have nuclear weapons not to build, acquire or possess nuclear weapons while obligating states that do have such weapons to not transfer them to other countries and to eventually disarm their nuclear facilities. Currently, there are 189 states that have signed this treaty. Of the eight states that have nuclear weapons, only the United States, Russia, the United Kingdom, France and China have signed this treaty while India, Pakistan and North Korea have yet to do so.[56]

Chemical and biological weapons: Currently, 188 states have signed the international Chemical Weapons Convention, also known as the Convention on the Prohibition, Production, Stockpiling and Use of Chemical Weapons and Their Destruction. As a result of this Convention, 60% of all declared chemical weapons have been destroyed. Parties to this treaty agree not to develop, produce, stockpile, or transfer chemical weapons – in any capacity. This convention has an effective, transparent compliance process, as countries are required to submit annual reports as well as undergo intrusive inspections with little notice.[57]

In 1972, the Biological and Toxin Weapons Convention (BTWC) was established to prohibit the use, possession, development, production and stockpiling of biological weapons and toxins. Currently, 163 states have signed this Convention, which has encountered difficult compliance issues. For example, several countries in the former U.S.S.R. continued to expand their biological weapon program despite signing this treaty. The production of biological weapons is hard to monitor because it does not require any particular start-up materials or facilities and the same start-up elements are often involved in food industry start-ups. In 2002, a compliance protocol was put into effect that requires parties to the BTWC to declare facilities capable of dual-use, and also requires random inspection of these facilities. The United States has not yet signed this compliance agreement, claiming that it aims to control the intellectual property rights of the country's biotech industry.[58]

Global citizens should investigate whether or not their country is a signatory to the convention and compliance provisions of the international agreements to prevent the spread of nuclear, chemical, and biological weapons. If your country is not a signatory, you should lobby or advocate for having your nation sign the agreement. There is also much that can be done to advocate for treaties that can further an ultimate goal of global disarmament. Global citizens can participate or help support organizations and activities, such as the Global Forum on Disarmament and Non-Proliferation Education, works towards this objective.

Questions for global citizens to address: What can be done to strengthen the effectiveness of global mechanisms to curb or eliminate weapons of mass destruction? What are their strengths? What are their limits? Has your country signed the international agreements to prevent the spread of nuclear, chemical and biological weapons? If not, why not, and what can you do to change your country's policy? How can you work with global citizens in other countries to advocate for better international agreements to control the spread of WMDs and destroy existing stockpiles?

- **GOVERNANCE ISSUES IN FAILED STATES AND COUNTRIES IN CONFLICT**

Those on the path to global citizenship cannot help but be aware of the growing number of war-torn countries, failed states, and nations emerging from conflict. Included in this list Afghanistan and East Timor in Asia, countries such as Sudan, Somalia, and the Congo in Africa, Chechnya and Kosovo in the Caucasus and Balkans, and Haiti in the Caribbean.

Failed states and war torn countries pose important questions for the international community. Whose responsibility are they? What can be done to help them settle their conflicts and re-establish essential systems of governance and public safety? Are these states viable as countries in the long-run, or do we need to look at alternative approaches that can help provide governance and stability to people living in them?

Because governments are often weak or because a new state must be constituted after violent hostilities cease, post-conflict countries usually need immediate assistance to restore governance and carry out the tasks of economic, political, physical, and political reconstruction. The United Nations, bilateral aid agencies, non-governmental organizations and others are needed to assist post-conflict countries to perform essential governance functions.

There are four different types of approaches to build governance capacity in failed or post-conflict states: (a) substituting an external authority for weak or yet to be constituted governments; (b) direct assistance to build the capacity of weak or fragile governments; (c) setting up semi-autonomous trust funds to manage aid and help strengthen government capacity; and (d) assistance through non-governmental organizations. The nature of the approach that is used will depend on the specific environment on the ground. Often the feasibility of interventions is limited by social, political, economic, and military conditions, and by the weak absorptive capacity of government. Proposed changes need to focus on increasing the capacity of government to perform those roles and functions that are most urgently needed.

As global citizens we need to reach out to those who live in failed states or post conflict countries to better understand their issues and needs. We then will be in a more informed position to advocate for whatever international measures may be needed to restore security and governance. The internet and other information technologies make communications with those living in conflict areas much more possible today than twenty or thirty years ago. The use of social networks, YouTube, blogs, and cell phones enable those trapped in conflict to communicate with the outside world.[59]

> **Global citizen issues:** Who should be responsible for trying to restore governance in failed states? How should decisions be made about which countries/organizations take responsibility? What are the strengths and limits of existing approaches to governance in

failed states and post conflict countries? Should failed states be preserved as states? How can the international community work more effectively to coordinate its support for failed states?

- ### THE PREVENTION AND MANAGEMENT OF WORLD HEALTH PANDEMICS

The worldwide transmission of infectious disease is another important issue about which global citizens need to be concerned. Today's increased ability of people today to travel and work in different countries also facilitates the spread of infectious diseases around the world. However our ability to identify and monitor epidemiological trends, as well as prevent and treat disease, help mitigate our increased risk. International organizations, such as the World Health Organization try to track the origins and spread of infectious diseases, prevent global pandemics, and facilitate the management of such pandemics when they occur. In recent years WHO has focused much of its work on the current pandemics of HIV and AIDS and influenza A/H1N1.

In most instances WHO relies on the voluntary cooperation of public health organizations in different countries, i.e. national and state health departments, medical research agencies, NGOs working in health, foundations, and others. There are only three diseases for which countries have established international health regulations ----yellow fever, plague, and cholera. For these three diseases binding international public health agreements require that countries provide WHO with immediate reports on all suspected cases and deaths related to the disease. For all other diseases, including HIV and AIDS, reporting requirements are nationally or sub-nationally determined. This introduces an element of non-comparability into global disease surveillance systems, since information on the same disease is collected in a somewhat different way depending on the country.[60]

The global health care professional community has an impressive track record in addressing the health care needs of those living in poverty, especially in developing countries. Organizations such as the U.S. Centers for Disease Control, the Carter Center, and the Clinton and Gates Foundations have worked to strengthen the ability of local public health institutions to prevent and treat infectious diseases such as river blindness, guinea worm, malaria, diarrhea, malnutrition, polio, measles, and tuberculosis. A recent focus of their efforts has been to work with private sector pharmaceutical companies to enable low-income families in developing countries to have greater access to immunizations and drug treatments.

Global citizens can contribute in a variety of ways to the many efforts going on around the world to prevent and treat infectious disease. We can work to strengthen international health policies of our governments and the global governance agencies, such as WHO that work in the field of public health. We can make donations to the many NGOs working in international health, or serve as a health NGO volunteer. We also can increase our awareness and practice of individual behaviors that help control pandemics, for example: by paying attention to global surveillance data from WHO and other health organizations; keeping informed about the symptoms of the disease; following WHO and government related health behavior guidelines; keeping up-to-date on vaccinations; practicing good general hygiene; and being ready and not worried and spreading fear and panic.[61]

Questions for global citizens to address: Does your country effectively collaborate and help support WHO and other international health organizations? In what ways should existing global public health governance mechanisms be strengthened? What can be done to promote greater access to drugs and health care services by families living in poverty in developing countries?

Chapter 8. TAKING ACTION

It used to be that the only meaningful way for an individual to influence global issues was through advocating for change in the foreign policies of their countries. While this remains a viable, and effective channel, a variety of other options are now available to those of us interested in changing the world. In Chapter 8 we describe four different ways in which we can voice our concerns, and help address the important political, economic, and social issues that affect the planet as a whole. These include becoming a global social entrepreneur, working to change the foreign policy of our countries, using philanthropy to change the polices of global governance institutions, using social media to promote global change and adapting sustainable environmental practices.

Becoming a global social entrepreneur: Those on the path to global citizenship may be interested in becoming global social entrepreneurs; launching activities that help solve global issues.   Social entrepreneurs are individuals with innovative solutions for society's most pressing problems. They are ambitious and persistent, tackling major issues and offering new ideas for wide-scale change. Rather than leaving societal needs to the government or business sector, social entrepreneurs find what is not working and solve the problem by changing the system.

Historical examples of famous global social entrepreneurs include Maria Montessori who developed and promoted the Montessori approach to early childhood education now widely used around the world; Florence Nightinggale, the founder of modern nursing, and Jean Monnet who helped establish the European Coal and Steel Community, precursor to the European Union.[62]

A contemporary example is 1997 Nobel Prize Winner, Jody Williams, who showed us how individual advocacy and intention can make a long-lasting difference in the world. Born and raised in Vermont, Ms. Williams began her career by teaching English as a Second Language (ESL) in Mexico and the United Kingdom. With an interest in Central America, Ms. Williams became involved with the Nicaragua-Honduras Education Project and then with a Los Angeles based non-profit organization, Medical Aid for El Salvador. During her time in Central America, she witnessed first hand the detrimental effects of landmines and the powerlessness that they presented to communities in crisis. In her Nobel Peace Prize Address she stated: "The land mine is eternally prepared to take victims.....The war ends, the land mine goes on killing."

In 1992 she helped establish the International Campaign to Ban Landmines (ICBL) and became its founding coordinator. The ICBL started out by conducting exhaustive research on landmines and their deadly effects. This work led them to spearhead an international advocacy campaign to develop an international treaty banning the use of landmines. In 1997 the campaign gained public support from Princess Diana of Wales. Later that year, on December of 1997, 122 nations signed the Ottowa Treaty banning the use of antipersonnel landmines, and in 1997, after the signing of the treaty, both Williams and the ICBL won the Nobel Peace Prize.[63]

Jody Williams utilized the power of people and technology to spread the zeal of her anti landmine transnational political movement. She utilized fax and later, email, to get people and organizations committed to making long-lasting change. Though she led this campaign, she could not have done it alone. By working with others, she was able to drive this campaign forward to such a degree that her actions resulted in international political change.

- **WORKING TO CHANGE THE FOREIGN POLICY OF YOUR STATE**

Every global citizen also is a citizen of his or her country; and, as such, can work to help make their nation's foreign policy more consistent with values of our emerging world community. This was the mission of Adam Sterling, an American college student who became impassioned about getting his home state of California to do something to address human rights abuses in the Sudan.

Thinking back to his days as a Junior at the University of California Los Angeles, Adam Sterling stated "I figured out how to walk through the entire campus without grabbing a single flier." He did not consider himself an activist, but rather, a normal college student trying to get by day-to-day. Out of curiosity he enrolled in an African Studies course where he learned about the 1994 Rwandan Genocide and the ongoing Genocide in Darfur.

When he thought of Genocide he thought of the Holocaust – an event that killed many of his family members and ravaged the world. He was shocked to learn how history repeated itself, over and over again. Sterling decided to start a Darfur advocacy group on campus with the aim of spreading awareness and education. Only four people showed up to the first meeting. Despite the small turnout, the group organized and began to make their presence known on campus. Sterling stated: " we wanted to be effective. We were ignorant and didn't know how difficult the bureaucracy would be. We didn't think we had that much influence and we looked for the people who did."[64]

After spending a significant amount of time researching the issue overseas foreign investment, Sterling learned that there were many multinational companies doing business with Sudan. The state of California had over $300 billion in overseas investments and part of that was going into companies doing work in Sudan. Sterling formulated a plan of action focused on getting the state to divest funds it was investing in their companies. In early 2006, he along with 200 other student activists bussed down to San Diego for a University of California Board of Regents meeting. Then, in March of 2006, the University of California system implemented a model of targeted divestment that focused on withdrawing funds from the worst offending companies doing business in Sudan. The UC system became the first public institution to take this kind of action. Later that year, Governor Schwarzenegger signed into law two Sudan divestment-related bills. His actions resulted in eight large international companies withdrawing from doing business in Sudan.

Following the success of the California Sudan divestment campaign, many institutions and legislators from other states began to contact Sterling with hopes of taking similar action. In response Sterling established the Sudan Divestment Task Force, a program that has successfully persuaded other universities, pension funds, and local, state and foreign governments to divest from companies working in or with Sudan.[65]

Sterling wasn't always an activist. He became motivated by what he learned in school, and channeled his anger, and passion in a manner that changed the foreign investment practices of his State. In the process he became a global citizen, partnered with others, and established a movement that has had an impact on an important world issue.

- **MAKING USE OF PHILANTHROPY CHANGE THE POLICIES OF GLOBAL GOVERNANCE ORGANIZATIONS**

In a time of diminishing budgets, global governance organizations have become interested in partnering with third parties who can provide them with much needed resource support. This has opened the door for partnerships with global citizen philanthropists who have an interest in strengthening or reforming global governance.

Recently the billionaire investor and philanthropist, Warren Buffet, pledged $50 million to help the U.N. Atomic Energy Agency (IEAE) set up a global nuclear fuel bank that aspiring nations can turn to for reactor fuel instead of making it themselves. The goal of Buffet's investment is to help reduce the risk of weapons proliferation by providing an alternative to national level production of nuclear fuel, which countries use to power either bombs or reactors. The new fuel bank also is seen as creating a global mechanism to aid the lighting of cities and hinder the means of destroying them. "I've never been $50 million lighter and felt better," Mr. Buffet said in an interview with the New York Times.[66]

In 1998 the entrepreneur and philanthropist, Ted Turner, established the United Nations Foundation with a $1 billion charitable donation. The UN Foundation is now a public charity that builds and implements public-private partnerships to address the world's most pressing problems, and broadens support for the UN through advocacy and public outreach.[67] If you visit the UN Foundation website there is a list of 154 private sector partner organizations ---- from the Belize Tourist Board to the Rockefeller Brothers Fund ---- that have contributed to the Foundation's efforts to strengthen the work of the United Nations.[68]

- **USING SOCIAL MEDIA TO PROMOTE GLOBAL CHANGE**

The recent events in Egypt, Tunisia and other parts of the Middle East demonstrate the power of social media, such as Facebook and Twitter, to mobilize large numbers of people for social change. Earlier examples in Serbia, Moldova, Iran Spain and the Philippines and other countries show how a networked population has an enhanced ability to undertake public action. In these and other countries people have used social media tools----such as text messaging, email. Photo sharing, and social networking----to communicate with one another and organize public gatherings in support of political and social change. These same tools can be used on a global scale. A networked population of global citizens could be mobilized to coordinate efforts in countries around the world on issues such as global warming, poverty reduction and weapons of mass destruction.

- **SUPPORTING CONSUMPTION PRACTICES THAT ARE ENVIRONMENTALLY SUSTAINABLE**

Another easily accessible way of fulfilling your responsibilities as a global citizen is by adapting environmentally friendly consumer practices. One way to do this is by joining the "fair trade" movement. The movement is an attempt to put an environmental framework around our quest for higher standards of living. The term "fair trade" refers to market-place exchanges that are done in a morally just and environmentally friendly manner. The Fair Trade Federation's 2005 Annual Report describes the movement as "a global network of producers, traders, marketers, advocates and consumers focused on building equitable trading relationships between consumers and the world's most economically disadvantaged artisans and farmers."[69] Fair trade practices work to alleviate poverty, improve working conditions, bring less strain to the environment and exchange goods in a manner that provides sustainability to this practice.

The story of the Toledo Cacao Growers Association in Belize (TCGA) is an example of how much Fair Trade makes a difference. The Association has 126 members, and was formed in 1986 in order to help its members get higher prices, improve the quality of their product, and improve their living conditions. Between 1992 and 1993 the world price of cocoa was suddenly cut in half, and many of the cooperative's members had to leave their crops un harvested. Fortunately, a chocolate company from the United Kingdom offered TCGA a long-term contract for a stable supply of quality cocoa at an above-market price. In 1998 TCGA produced 28.6 tons of organic cocoa beans and in 1999 22.2 tons, all of which were sold through the Fair Trade market.[70]

Another environmentally sustainable consumption practice, followed by global citizens in Europe, is the movement towards 'eco-labeling' or 'environmental labeling.'
This movement promotes "the voluntary granting of labels in order to inform consumers and thereby promote consumer products which are determined to be environmentally more friendly than other more functionally and competitively similar products." Examples of Eco labels are Germany's 'Blue Angel'-the first Eco labeling scheme introduced in the late 1970s; the 'Nordic Swan' and the EU 'Flower.' Eco-labeled products include batteries, detergents, clothing,

building materials, compost, eggs, meat, vegetables, home appliances, and paper products.[71] In

Sweden products with at least 25% greenhouse gas savings will be marked in each food

category, starting with plant production, dairy and fish products.[72]

PART III: GLOBAL GOVERNANCE

Chapter 9. ORGANIZATIONAL PROFILES

Global citizens need to understand as much as possible about the workings of global governance organizations. These institutions establish standards and make rules and regulations that affect the character of our world community.

Our globalized world, with its increasingly integrated economic markets, has made it difficult for nation states to exercise their customary degree of sovereign control. No government today can impose enduring restrictions on commerce, capital, and communications unless it wants to end up being in a state of international isolation. It must, however reluctantly, cede control for certain functions to institutions with global governance responsibilities.

Global governance is defined as the collective management of common problems at the international level.[73] Traditionally global governance mechanisms, such as the United Nations, have been established by politicians, diplomats, and international civil servants. But in the age of global citizenships, non-state actors, such as NGOs and professional associations, have moved to provide global governance functions in areas of perceived need. Those on the path to global citizenship should keep a careful eye on the operation of global governance organizations. Many are run by oversized bureaucracies, and suffer from a lack of transparency and accountability.

This chapter provides brief profiles of different types of global governance institutions, their strengths and limitations. Organizations profiled include the United Nations; international courts; global economic management institutions; international agencies that regulate the use of weapons of mass destruction; international law enforcement organizations; global professional associations, ; regional governance organizations; networks of countries with industrial and emerging economies; multinational corporations and global governance watchdog organizations.

We also offer suggestions as to ways in which those on the path to global citizenship can help support these organizations and/or monitor their performance. It is worth noting that, as individual citizens, we lack direct access to most global governance institutions. This is largely because global governance institutions have been established by national governments to carry out functions that individual nations cannot implement on their own. Therefore managers of global governance institutions report to representatives from the countries empowering and funding their institution to do its work. They are not accountable directly to "the people."

The United Nations

192 countries -- nearly every nation on the planet -- are members of the United Nations. The U.N. Charter, the organization's founding document, was originally written in 1945 by the representatives of 50 different countries. The Charter provides for an organization managed by six administrative organs, the two most important being the General Assembly and the Security

Council. (The other four are the Economic and Social Council, the Secretariat, the International Court of Justice, and the United Nations Trusteeship Council.)Other prominent UN System agencies include the World Health Organization (WHO), the Food and Agriculture Organization (FAO), the World Food Programme (WFP), and the United Nations Children's Fund (Unicef).

Some experts challenge the specialized nature of the UN agencies. They assert that an international system based on "specialized agencies" is not the best fit for a world struggling to address interconnected issues. While the 20th century relied on specialists, the 21st century may come to rely more on people who are integrationists, capable within their expertise but excelling in their grasp of the relationship between their area of expertise and those adjacent to it.[74]

In the U.N. General Assembly every country gets one vote. Any "important question" for the General Assembly requires a two-thirds majority for approval. According to the U.S. State Department, "important questions" include: recommendations on peace and security; election of members to organs; admission, suspension, and expulsion of members; and budgetary issues. All other matters are decided with a simple majority.

U.N. Members confer on the Security Council primary responsibility for the maintenance of international peace and security, and agree that in carrying out its duties under this responsibility the Security Council acts on their behalf. The Security council has five permanent members (Britain, China, France, Russia, and the United States) and 10 members elected by the general assembly that serve two-year terms (currently Angola, Bulgaria, Cameroon, Chile, Germany, Guinea, Mexico, Pakistan, Spain and Syria). On important matters, it is necessary to get nine members of the Security Council to agree. However the five permanent members each have veto power, and any one of them can block any resolution of the Security Council.

Funding for the U.N. comes from the member nations. The General Assembly is in charge of ratifying a budget, developed by the Secretary General, and deciding how much money each nation will pay into the system. Money gets divided into three functional areas: the normal U.N. operating budget; the peacekeeping budget; and voluntary contributions, mostly for humanitarian efforts.[75]

At one time the United Nations represented the world's best hope for promoting international cooperation and the peaceful resolution of disputes between countries. However today the UN is struggling to remain relevant on the world stage.. "A lot of the juice is outside the United Nations," says Bruce Jones, the Director of the Center for International Cooperation at New York University. "The old days when the US and Europeans could stitch things up at the United Nations are over."[76]

It has been difficult for the U.N. to resolve the ideological debate among its members between those who argue that the international community has the right to intervene to prevent mass atrocities and those who believe that the concept of state sovereignty, recognized in the United

Nations Charter is sacrosanct. However, recently there has been an emerging consensus among Security Council members about the need to take action to prevent violence against civilians. In 2005 the organization passed a resolution to help the U.N. intervene to stop the threat of genocide. The New York Times quotes Stephani Crouzat, spokesman for the French mission to the U.N. as saying that ' There is a new trend in the Security Council in which the responsibility to protect principle is gaining a new hold.' Invoking past conflicts in Rwanda, Darfur, and Bosnia, he adds that 'There is a desire to intervene before war crimes or ethnic cleansing can take place.'[77]

Since its founding there have been many calls for reform of the United Nations, although little consensus on how to do so. The U.N. has been accused of bureaucratic inefficiency and waste. During the 1990s, the United States withheld dues citing inefficiency, and only started repayment on the condition that a major reforms initiative was introduced. In 1994, the Office of Internal Oversight Services was established by the General Assembly to serve as an efficiency watchdog. There also have been numerous calls for the U.N. Security Council's membership to be increased, for different ways of electing the UN's Secretary General, and for a United Nations Parliamentary Assembly.

Opportunities for Global Citizens: There are few direct access channels open to global citizens interested in participating in a United Nations decision-making process. Individuals interested in making their voices known on a particular U.N. issue can either work through their country's U.N. representative or help organize a U.N. petition drive. Many U.N. member countries have national United Nations Associations. These organizations provide an opportunity for global citizens to become involved in creating greater awareness in our countries about the work that the U.N. does, and advocating to have our countries provide greater resource support for the U.N. In addition, global citizens may want to engage with organizations that are trying to improve the U.N. system's effectiveness and efficiency.

INTERNATIONAL COURTS : THE INTERNATIONAL COURT OF JUSTICE (THE WORLD COURT) AND THE INTERNATIONAL CRIMINAL COURT

- ### THE INTERNATIONAL COURT OF JUSTICE (WORLD COURT)

The International Court of Justice is the principal judicial organ of the United Nations, established by chapter 14 of the U.N. Charter. The Court's role is to settle legal disputes submitted to it by States and to give advisory opinions on legal questions referred to it by authorized United Nations organs and specialized agencies. The court has 15 judges chosen by the General Assembly and the Security Council from a list of candidates nominated by government-appointed national groups of international-law experts. No two judges may be from the same country. Nine judges constitute a quorum, and questions are decided by a majority of the judges present. All members of the United Nations are members of the court; other states may adhere to the statute.

Concern has been expressed at the small number of cases nations have submitted to the court. Major opinions of the court have ruled that the General Assembly may not admit a state to the United Nations if the application is vetoed by one of the permanent members of the Security

Council; that the United Nations is to be considered as an international legal person; and that special United Nations assessments, such as those for the Congo and Middle East operations, are regular expenses of the United Nations and are binding on all members.[78]

Opportunities for Global Citizen Participation: There are limited opportunities for direct participation since cases brought before the court must come from member states or from the United Nations. To our knowledge individual citizens are not allowed to be cited as plaintiffs or defendants .If you are a member of the legal profession in your country you may have an opportunity to nominate judges for the court or be one yourself. You also may also have knowledge of the operations of the court, and be able to advise the rest of us on the court's effectiveness.

- ### INTERNATIONAL CRIMINAL COURT

The International Criminal Court, commonly referred to as the ICC is a permanent tribunal to prosecute individuals for genocide, crimes against humanity, war crimes, and the crime of aggression . Many states wanted to add terrorism and drug trafficking to the list of crimes covered by the ICC; however, countries were unable to agree on a definition for terrorism and it was decided not to include drug trafficking as this might overwhelm the court's limited resources. India lobbied to have the use of nuclear weapons and other weapons of mass destruction included as war crimes but this move was also defeated.

The creation of the ICC perhaps constitutes the most significant reform of international law since 1945. It gives teeth to the two bodies of international law that deal with treatment of individuals: human rights and humanitarian law. The court came into being on 1 July 2002—the date its founding treaty, the Rome Statute of the International Criminal Court, entered into force. It can only prosecute crimes committed on or after that date.

As of August 2010, 111 states are members of the Court. A further 35 countries, including Russia and the United States have signed but not ratified the Rome Statute. A number of states, including China and India, are critical of the court and have not signed the Rome Statute.[79]

The ICC can generally exercise jurisdiction only in cases where the accused is a national of a state party, the alleged crime took place on the territory of a state party, or a situation is referred to the court by the United Nations Security Council.

The court is presided over by 18 judges. Judges are elected to the court by member states. They serve nine-year terms and are not generally eligible for re-election. All judges must be nationals of states that have signed the Rome Statute, and no two judges may be nationals of the same state. They must be "persons of high moral character, impartiality and integrity who possess the qualifications required in their respective States for appointment to the highest judicial offices."

To date, the court has opened investigations into five situations: Northern Uganda, the Democratic Republic of the Congo, the Central African Republic, Darfur (Sudan), and the

Republic of Kenya. The court has indicted sixteen people; seven of whom remain fugitives, two have died (or are believed to have died), four are in custody, and three have appeared voluntarily before the court.[80]

Opportunities for global citizen participation: One of the great innovations of the International Criminal Court is the series of rights granted to victims. For the first time in the history of international criminal justice, victims have the possibility to present their views and observations before an international court. The victim-based provisions within the Rome Statute provide people with the opportunity to have their voices heard and obtain, where appropriate, some form of reparation for their suffering.

GLOBAL ECONOMIC MANAGEMENT INSTITUTIONS: THE INTERNATIONAL MONETARY FUND (IMF): THE WORLD BANK, AND THE WORLD TRADE ORGANIZATION (WTO)

- ### THE INTERNATIONAL MONETARY FUND (IMF)

The International Monetary Fund (IMF) is an organization of 187 countries, working to foster global monetary cooperation. The mission of the IMF is to help ensure stability in the international financial system. It does so in three ways: keeping track of the global economy and the economies of member countries; lending to countries with balance of payments difficulties; and giving practical help to members.

The IMF provides loans to countries that have trouble meeting their international payments and cannot otherwise find sufficient financing on affordable terms. This financial assistance is designed to help countries restore macroeconomic stability by rebuilding their international reserves, stabilizing their currencies, and paying for imports—all necessary conditions for launching growth. The IMF also provides concessional loans to low-income countries to help them develop their economies and reduce poverty.

The Board of Governors is the highest decision-making body of the IMF. The Board is composed of one governor and one alternate governor for each member country. The governor is appointed by the member country and is usually the minister of finance or the head of the central bank. A 24-member Executive Board, representing all 187-member countries, oversees the IMF's operations. Large economies, such as the United States and China, have their own seat on the Executive Board, but most countries are grouped in constituencies representing 4 or more countries.

Part of the global community believes that the IMF and its sister organization the World Bank are not open to hearing outside criticism of their policies. Critics of the Bank and the IMF believe that by "elevating concerns about macroeconomic financial stability above all other competing values, the institutions have created a human rights catastrophe; that force countries to cut social spending on health, education, and other public services, and demand that countries keep their wage levels artificially low." Since 1976, at least 100 protests against Fund and Bank policies have occurred in dozens of countries around the world.[81]

The IMF and the World Bank have taken steps to address these concerns. Whether they have gone far enough is a subject open to debate. Global citizens can and should have differences of opinion on this issue. We don't all need to speak with one voice all the time. However, when differences of opinion do exist, our community needs to bring all sides together, identify points of agreement, and promote respect for differing points of view.

Opportunities for global citizen participation: If you believe that the policies of the IMF and/or the World Bank are detrimental to human rights and social issues, you can join or help support NGOs that are working to change IMF policies, such as Global Exchange. If you want to have input on an IMF policy or advocate for the IMF to take a particular position on an issue, you can contact the office of your country's representative on the Bank's Board of Governors.

- **THE WORLD BANK**

The World Bank is a source of financial and technical assistance to developing countries around the world. Its mission is to fight poverty and help people help themselves by providing resources, sharing knowledge, building capacity and forging partnerships in the public and private sectors.

The World Bank provides low-interest loans, interest-free credits and grants to developing countries that support efforts in a variety of sectors including education, health, public administration, infrastructure, financial and private sector development, agriculture and the environment.[82]

The Bank seeks to make investments in projects that can directly benefit the poorest people in developing countries. The direct involvement of the poorest in economic activity is being promoted through lending for agriculture and rural development, small-scale enterprises, and urban development. The Bank seeks to help poor communities become more productive and to gain access to such necessities as safe water and waste-disposal facilities, health care, family-planning assistance, nutrition, education, and housing.

With over 7,000 staff members, the World Bank is about three times as large as the IMF, and maintains about 40 offices throughout the world, although 95 percent of its staff work at its Washington, D.C., headquarters. The Bank is accountable to its membership of 187 countries. Member states are represented by a Board of Governors, who are the Bank's ultimate policy makers. Generally, the governors are member countries' ministers of finance or ministers of development. They meet once a year at the Annual Meetings of the Boards of Governors of the World Bank Group and the International Monetary Fund. Because the governors only meet annually, they delegate specific duties to 24 Executive Directors, who work on-site at the Bank. Each of the five largest shareholders, France, Germany, Japan, the United Kingdom and the United States appoint an Executive Director, while other member countries are represented by 19 executive directors.

The President of the World Bank, reports to the Executive Directors Board, and is responsible for overall management of the Bank. By tradition, the Bank President is a U.S. national and is nominated by the United States, the Bank's largest shareholder. The Executive Directors select the President, from a list of those nominated by the Bank's member counties. The President serves for a five-year, renewable term.[83]

Opportunities for global citizen participation: In the face of popular criticism that it was a top down institution, the World Bank in recent years has instituted a variety of formal community consultation processes. These processes are designed to help ensure that communities affected by Bank projects have an opportunity to contribute to and review the ways in which projects are designed and implemented. Affected communities are now required to be consulted on Bank project related environmental assessments, environmental management plans, resettlement action plans, indigenous peoples plans, and pest management plans. Those consulted include project beneficiaries, project-affected people, and other interested parties, such as local governments and NGOs.

- **WORLD TRADE ORGANIZATION**

The mission of the World Trade Organization (WTO) is to supervise and liberalize international trade. The organization was launched on January 1, 1995 under the international Marrakech Agreement, which replaced the General Agreement on Tariffs and Trade (GATT). WTO deals with the regulation of trade between participating countries; it provides a framework for negotiating and formalizing trade agreements, facilitates the establishment of such agreements, and manages a dispute resolution process for issues related to participants' adherence to WTO agreements.

WTO has 153 members, which are responsible for more than 97% of world trade. In addition there are 30 observer nations seeking membership. WTO is governed by (a) economic development and trade ministers from member countries who meet every two years; (b) a general council, which implements the conference's policy decisions; and (c) a Director-General, responsible for organizational management who is appointed by the ministerial conference.[84]

WTO operates on a *one country, one vote* system, but actual votes have never been taken. Decision making is generally by consensus, and relative market size is the primary source of bargaining power. The advantage of consensus decision-making is that it encourages efforts to find the most widely acceptable decision. The main disadvantages of this process include the large time requirements and many rounds of negotiation needed to develop a consensus decision, and the tendency for final agreements to use ambiguous language on contentious points that make future interpretations difficult.

In reality, WTO negotiations proceed not by consensus of all members, but by a process of informal negotiations between small groups of countries. Such negotiations are often called

"Green Room" negotiations (after the color of the WTO Director-General's Office in Geneva), or "Mini-Ministerials", when they occur in other countries. These processes have been regularly criticized by many of the WTO's developing country members which are often excluded from the negotiations.

Globalization activists decry the WTO as being undemocratic. They believe that WTO rules are unduly influenced by industry groups who lobby with their country's WTO representative. They claim that citizen input by consumer, environmental, human rights, and labor organizations is consistently ignored. Activists also complain that WTO sponsored trade agreements ignore and rights of workers and basic human rights. They believe that WTO's commitment to the principles of free trade results in increased inequality, hurts poor countries, and is harmful to the environment. They argue that WTO needs to take into account human and social development factors, such as worker's rights, child labor, the protection of small -scale producers, and environmental protection.

Opportunities for global citizen participation: If you are in agreement with the globalization critics of WTO you can join or help support several of the NGOs which are sponsoring citizen action to change the organization's policies, such as United for a Fair Economy. If you work for a business, affected by WTO decisions, you can advocate for your position on issues that affect you by contacting your country's representative to the WTO.

INTERNATIONAL AGENCIES THAT REGULATE OF WEAPONS OF MASS DESTRUCTION

• **INTERNATIONAL ATOMIC ENERGY AGENCY**

The International Atomic Energy Agency (IAEA) promotes the peaceful use of nuclear energy, and seeks to inhibit its use for any military purpose, including nuclear weapons. The IAEA provides an intergovernmental forum for scientific and technical cooperation in the peaceful use of nuclear technology and nuclear power worldwide. The programs of the IAEA encourage the development of peaceful applications of nuclear technology, provide international safeguards against misuse of nuclear technology and nuclear materials, and promote nuclear safety (including radiation protection) and nuclear security standards and their implementation.

151 countries currently belong to the IAEA. The IAEA governance structure includes a 35 member Board of Governors and a General Conference of all members. The Board, in its five yearly meetings, is responsible for making most of the policy decisions of the IAEA.

As an independent international organization related to the United Nations, the IAEA´s relationship with the U.N. is regulated by special agreement . The IAEA submits annual reports to the U.N. General Assembly and the Security Council regarding non-compliance by States with their treaty obligations as well as on matters relating to international peace and security.

A major responsibility of IAEA is to monitor the implementation of the international Treaty on the Non-Proliferation of Nuclear Weapons, also known as the Nuclear Non-Proliferation Treaty (NPT or NNPT).The treaty came into effect on March 5th 1970. Currently there are 189 states which have signed the treaty, five of whom are recognized as nuclear weapon states: the United States, Russia, the United Kingdom, France, and China (These countries also are the five permanent members of the United Nations Security Council.).

Countries signing the NPT agree not to "receive," "manufacture" or "acquire" nuclear weapons or "seek or receive any assistance in the manufacture of nuclear weapons" . They also agree to accept monitoring by the International Atomic Energy Agency (IAEA) to verify that they are not diverting nuclear energy from peaceful uses to nuclear weapons or other nuclear explosive devices."

Under the NPT the five nuclear weapon states agree not to transfer "nuclear weapons or other nuclear explosive devices" and "not in any way to assist, encourage, or induce" a non-nuclear weapon state to acquire nuclear weapons.[85]

Four non-parties to the treaty are known or believed to possess nuclear weapons: India, Israel, Pakistan and North Korea. India, Pakistan and North Korea have declared that they possess nuclear weapons, while Israel has had a policy of deliberate ambiguity regarding its own nuclear weapons program. North Korea acceded to the treaty, violated it, and in 2003 withdrew from its signature.

Opportunities for global citizen participation: There is little opportunity for global citizens to have direct input into the decisions of the IAEA, except perhaps by lobbying with a member of the Board of Governors who represents your country. Those interested in protesting an IAEA policy can work through their country's representative to the U.N., where such policies are often discussed. There also is an interesting example of how a citizen / philanthropist can affect IAEA policies and programs. Warren Buffet, the billionaire philanthropist recently donated $50,000,0000 to help the IAEA establish a Global Nuclear Fuel Bank (For more on this see Chapter 6).

INTERNATIONAL LAW ENFORCEMENT ORGANIZATIONS

- **INTERPOL**

The mission of the International Criminal Police Organization (INTERPOL) is to enhance cooperation among member countries and stimulate the exchange of information between all national and international law enforcement bodies concerned with countering organized crime groups and related corruption. 188 countries are members of INTERPOL, which has an annual budget $59 million and a staff of 588 people.

INERPOL's General Assembly is composed of delegates appointed by the governments of member countries. As INTERPOL's supreme governing body, the Assembly meets once a year and takes all major decisions affecting general policy, the resources needed for international co-operation, working methods, finances and programmes of activities. The Assembly makes decisions by a simple majority in the form of resolutions. Each Member country represented

has one vote. (1)

INTERPOL differs from most law-enforcement agencies. Agents do not make arrests

themselves, and there is no single INTERPOL jail where criminals are taken. The agency

functions as an administrative liaison between the law enforcement agencies of its member

countries, providing communications and database assistance. This is vital when fighting

international crime because language, cultural and bureaucratic differences make it difficult for

officers from different nations to work together.[86]

In the event of an international disaster, terrorist attack, or assassination, INTERPOL usually

sends an incident response team. This team assists with victim identification, suspect

identification, and the dissemination of information to other nations' law enforcement agencies.

In addition, at the request of local authorities, INTERPOL response teams can act as a central

command and logistics operation to coordinate other law enforcement agencies involved in the

case.

In order to maintain as politically neutral a role as possible, INTERPOL's constitution forbids its

involvement in any political, military, religious or racial crimes. Its work focuses primarily on

public safety, terrorism, organized crime, crimes against humanity, environmental crime,

genocide, war crimes, piracy, illicit drug production, drug trafficking, weapons smuggling, human trafficking, money laundering, child pornography, white collar crime, computer crime, intellectual property crime, and corruption.[87]

Critics of INTERPOL claim that allowing foreign police officers to actively hunt for criminals in another country constitutes a violation of national sovereignty. They also point to some INTERPOL member countries whose law enforcement and judicial systems are highly suspect, such as Venezuela, Saudi Arabia, Sudan, Iran, Cuba, Somalia, and Yemen.[88]

Opportunities for global citizen participation: If you are a member of a national or local law enforcement agency (LEA), and your country is a member of INTERPOL, you most likely can have input into the agency's policies and services. You would need to communicate your suggestions through your country's representative to INTERPOL General Assembly.

INTERNATIONAL PROFESSIONAL ASSOCIATIONS

Membership in international professional associations provide global citizens with perhaps the most direct access that is available to them for participation in a global governance organization. If you are a member of a profession that has an international association, you have an opportunity to participate in the setting of global standards and regulations for your profession. All sorts of professions --- from accountants to zoo-keepers---now have international associations that share best practice and establish standards and regulations to help guide the work being done in their fields. Several examples of how international professional associations provide a global governance function were described in Chapter 4.

REGIONAL GOVERNANCE ORGANIZATIONS AND ASSOCIATIONS

Regional organizations and associations have an important role to play in the governance of the political, economic and social sectors in the parts of the world where they operate. There is wide variation in the structure and function of regional governance organizations.

The most relevant model for the establishment of a regional federation of states is the European Union (EU), which politically unites a large group of widely diverse, some formerly hostile, nations spread over a large geographic area and 500 million people. Though the EU is still evolving, it already has many attributes of a federal government, such as open internal borders, a directly elected parliament, a court system, an official currency (Euro) and a centralized economic policy.[89]

Elsewhere, a multitude of regional associations are in different stages of development along a continuum of economic and sometimes political integration. These include the Caribbean Community (CARICOM), African Union (AU), the Association of Southeast Asian Nations (ASEAN), the Shanghai Cooperation Organization, Commonwealth of Independent States, Arab League, Union of South American Nations, the South Asian Association for Regional Cooperation, and the Organization of the Islamic Conference.[90]

A key question questions for global citizens is whether regional organizations will prove to be a building block for, or a drain on global governance. In the former case, regional cooperation would be complimentary to and compatible with broader multilateral agreements, for example in the field of peacekeeping. In the latter case, the investment in regional cooperation might detract from the goal of strengthening global governance frameworks, in the area of international trade for example.

Regional cooperation has not so far resulted in a significant pooling or delegation of sovereignty. In most cases, regional governance frameworks uphold the principle of non-interference in the internal affairs of member states.

Opportunities for global citizen participation: The European Union has made a large-scale commitment to encouraging citizen participation in governance. The EU's Europe for Citizens Programme aims to give the citizen a key role in the development of the EU. Over a seven-year period, Europe for Citizens will focus on four key actions to bring about change: *active citizenship for Europe,* which aims to bring people from different parts of Europe together to promote mutual understanding, a sense of ownership of the EU, and the emergence of a European identity; *active civil society in Europe* which seeks to help European civil society play a more active role on the European stage; *together in Europe,* which organizes high profile events to help people realize that values can be shared across borders; and *active Europe remembrance,* which seeks to keep painful memories of Nazism and Stalinism alive in order to provide lessons on the value of today's peace, stability and democracy in Europe.[91]

Since 1973, the world's industrial powers have organized themselves into semi-formal networks for the purposes of exchanging information, coordinating policies, and influencing the actions of other countries. The first such network was called the G-6 and consisted of the Heads of State of France, West Germany, Italy, Japan, the United Kingdom, and the United States. Canada joined the Group in 1976 making it the G 7, and Russia joined in 1997 making it the G 8. Together the countries of the G 8 represent about 14% of the world's population and 60% of the Gross World Product.[92]

The Group of Twenty (G 20) was established in 1999 to bring together Finance Ministers and Central Bank Governors from leading industrialized and developing economies to discuss key issues in the global economy. It also has helped coordinate economic growth policies and efforts to combat terrorist financing. The G 20 has held major meetings to help coordinate member responses to global financial crisis, such as those in 199 and in 2007-2008. Members include Argentina, Australia, Brazil, Canada, China, France, Germany, India, Indonesia, Italy, Japan, Mexico, Russia, Saudi Arabia, South Africa, Republic of Korea, Turkey, United Kingdom, and United States of America.[93]

By design the G 8 and the G 20 deliberately lack an administrative structure. They do not have a permanent secretariat or offices for their members. The presidency, and responsibility for planning meetings, rotates annually among member countries.

Industrial and emerging economy networks, such as the G 8 and G 20, put an emphasis on the networked coordination of member states. The decisions of their forums are of a political nature and non-binding. The development of the 'Gs' responds to two basic needs: the need to foster collective leadership to jointly address shared problems outside the constraints imposed by formal multilateral structures, and secondly, the need for inter-state networks that reflect the changing balance of world power.

Networks, such as the G 8 and G 20, may be increasingly called upon to set the direction for international cooperation on important global issues, and serve as top-level international agenda setting bodies. For example, during the 2007/2008 global financial crisis the G-20 called on the IMF and World Bank to monitor relevant national policy measures and lend financial support to countries in need. In the energy sector the G-20 promoted closer cooperation between the International Atomic Energy Agency (IAEA), OPEC, OECD, and the World Bank.

Industrial and emerging economy networks have faced growing criticism from human rights, labor, and environmental organizations. The most widespread criticisms center on the assertion that network members, especially the G 8, are responsible for exacerbating global problems, such as poverty and global warming. During the 31st G 8 summit in the United Kingdom, 225,000 people took to the streets calling for trade justice, debt relief, and better aid to developing countries.[94]

Opportunities for global citizen participation: Participation in G 8 and G 20 meetings tend to be reserved for heads of state and finance ministers. Citizens would have to lobby with their government representatives in order to have input into a G 8 or G 20 agenda (a challenging task to say the least). On the other hand, NGOs and community-based groups organizing efforts to protest G 8 and G 20 activities would welcome individual citizen involvement and support.

TRANSNATIONAL CORPORATIONS

The scale and pace of activities of transnational corporations are the focus of many major global governance issues. Although these companies do not directly implement global governance activities, the ways in which they do business has a profound impact on issues such as international trade, climate change, and human rights.

Ann Florini, a Senior Fellow at the Brookings Institute, notes: "The lack of effective international (and national) regulation to protect workers, communities and the environment has spurred the development of a powerful movement aimed at promoting corporate social responsibility, whose partisans have on occasion forced significant changes in business practices through campaigns aimed at consumers and investors. And because unregulated business activities can cause societies to question the legitimacy of corporations, corporate leaders themselves are struggling with fundamental questions about how far their social responsibilities extend, e.g. to shareholders, employees, local communities where they work, humanity as a whole?"[95]

Today many companies are creating "codes of conduct" to reassure consumers that their production processes are environmentally benign and that working conditions are decent. For example, Starbucks Coffee, faced with intense picketing by activists denouncing conditions at the Guatemalan coffee plantations where it purchases beans, has issued a code of conduct and action plans for all its suppliers.

The nonprofit Council on Economic Priorities, in collaboration with human rights organizations, businesses, and auditing companies, devised a code of conduct called Social Accountability 8000, intended to become the gold standard on workers' rights. Companies that adopt the code permit outside auditors to inspect every facility and assess practices on child labor, health and safety, freedom of association, the right to collective bargaining, discrimination, disciplinary practices, working hours, and whether compensation provides workers a living wage.

The U.N., under Secretary-General Kofi Annan, promulgated a "Global Compact" which asked corporations to indicate voluntary adherence to U.N. principles on human rights, labor standards, and the environment. Signatories are required to report annually on progress in implementing these principles.[96]

Increasing numbers of transnational corporations are agreeing to adopt codes of conduct, such as the "Global Compact" because of their need to please ever more highly aware investors, as well as consumers. Around the world growing numbers of people are adding social responsibility to their criteria for selecting companies in which to invest.

Opportunities for global citizen participation: Global citizens can influence the behavior of transnational corporation by engaging in direct action campaigns such boycotting the purchase of products from companies that lack or fail to adhere to ethical business practices. We also can avoid investing as shareholders in these companies, and participate and raise issues at shareholder meetings.

GLOBAL GOVERNANCE WATCH-DOG ORGANIZATIONS

There is a growing body of academic literature that analyzes trends and models of global governance. However, given the relative newness of global governance institutions, there have yet to be many organizations concerned with monitoring their performance.

The UK based One World Trust has established a Global Accountability Project Framework which provides a Framework for analyzing how global governance organizations can improve accountability to their stakeholders. This Framework unpacks accountability into four dimensions-*transparency, compliance and response, participation, and evaluation.* A responsive organization needs to integrate all four dimensions of accountability into its policies, procedures and practice. Each year One World Trust uses this framework to measure the performance of three different types of global governance organizations – intergovernmental bodies, such as UN agencies; transnational corporations, and international NGOs. For 2008, the last year when a One World Trust Accountability Report is available on the internet, the International Federation of Organic Agriculture Movements (IFOAM) received the highest scoring for an international NGO; the European Bank for Reconstruction and Development (EBRD) the highest score for an intergovernmental organization; and BHP Billiton the highest score in the corporate sector.[97]

Chapter 10. THE GOVERNANCE OF GLOBAL GOVERNANCE

For the foreseeable future nation states most likely will remain the principle unit that bestows legitimacy on the world's global governance institutions. However nation states, acting by themselves, lack the ability to adequately address the growing number of important issues, such as those described in Chapter 9 above, that affect the planet as a whole. Domestic politics often constrain international cooperation and reduce the scope for compromise.

Conflicts between and among states often arise when the interest of a nation state conflicts with the interests of the world as a whole. For example, the United States and other industrialized countries contributed over 60 % of the world's greenhouse gas emissions, and yet developing countries bear the biggest costs of environmental pollution. The policies of China and other countries in keeping the value of their currency artificially low, in order to support their export oriented economy, tends to distort world trade. Such policies hurt the economies of other countries by limiting their access to markets in China for imported goods and services.

Colin Bradford from the Brookings Institution makes the observation that: "The central challenge of the 21st century is that the institutional framework for dealing with contemporary global challenges does not match the scope, scale, and nature of the challenges themselves. This doesn't mean that the nation-state needs to be superseded by a better and stronger set of international institutions. To the contrary, the nation-state and national political leaders constitute the foundation of political legitimacy necessary for global governance and international institutional reform to move forward."[98]

Mr. Bradford's initial statement, about the lack of an institutional framework for dealing with contemporary global challenges, is an accurate one. But to what extent can we agree with his conclusion? Is the nation state the sole source of the "political legitimacy" needed to support global governance?

The nation state is a temporary flagship for global governance legitimacy. Its function in conveying such legitimacy is a carryover from the last century when nation-states were self-contained units that only cooperated with other units if it was mutually convenient for them to do so. However, global issues facing the world today require more than just existential agreements of convenience between countries. They require a more fundamental commitment to develop and support solutions that work for the planet as a whole.

The legitimacy of having global governance organizations be managed by a collection of sovereign states is further challenged by the variation in the ways these states themselves are governed. A survey by Freedom House that classifies countries in terms of the degree of individual liberty that their citizens enjoy, indicates that there are *89 free countries, 62 partly free countries and 42 not free countries.* The *not free countries* account for 34% of the world's 6.8 billion people, and include military dictatorships, repressive monarchies, countries with dominant political parties, and those with foreign occupiers ruling them. Given this variation in governing systems and principles of sovereign states, one must question to what degree they collectively represent the same constituency; and to what extent international politics and agreements make strange bedfellows.[99]

There is potentially a deeper source of legitimacy for the institutions of global governance. This comes from the values and principles of global citizens and our emerging world community. We have discussed these values in earlier chapters of this book. They include a commitment to basic human rights, protecting and sustaining the earth's ecosystem, and upholding the principle of open and participatory governance at all levels.

NGOs have important roles to play in making global governance more participatory. NGOs can give voice to citizens' concerns and channel them into the deliberative processes of international global governance organizations. Civil society organizations also can make the internal processes of global governance organizations more transparent to the wider public and formulate technical issues in accessible terms. They also can ensure that citizens' concerns are reflected in the decision-making processes of global governance institutions.[100]

Global governance institutions need to find ways to more directly engage with the citizens they serve. Mechanisms for direct citizen accountability of global governance institutions are at present quite weak, if they exist at all. A dialogue needs to take place to bridge the accountability gap between citizens and global governance institutions, perhaps initiated by the institutions perhaps by citizens themselves. Such a dialogue should include all major stakeholder groups with a vested stake in global governance----citizens groups, NGOs, transnational corporations, faith-based organizations, professional associations as well as representatives from nation states, participating as one among equals.

CHAPTER 11. WHAT HISTORY TEACHES US

Efforts to promote global governance and citizenship span a large swath of history -----from Alexander the Great in 356 BC through the founding of the United Nations in 1945. It is worth noting that most historical efforts have taken a top-down approach; that is they have begun with the establishment of top down governance frameworks; usually empires with associated legal codes, regulations, and policing mechanisms, and then tried to impose their ideas and systems on lands that were conquered.

It also is worth noting that most of these historical models are not ones that that those of us on the path to global citizenship would choose to emulate. We study them in large part because they teach us how <u>not</u> to go about the task of organizing global citizenship. All of them, with the exception of the United Nations, have eventually collapsed of their own weight.

Those who set out to establish world empires usually fail to learn the lessons of history, that all empires and nations and their leaders fall prey to their own narcissistic hubris and that all eventually collapse from within.(1) Is this cycle of growth and decay built into our DNA, or is there any way that we can learn from it and avoid its trap? We are at an interesting time in history when there is no world empire per say. Experts say that we are at the end of an era of American dominance. If this is so then what comes next? Some say that the new millennium will be a time of dominance by China and India, but is this a foregone conclusion? Do the forces we have been speaking about in this book portend a different approach to the way in which the world will evolve?[101]

This chapter offers a short survey of major historical efforts to establish global governance. The examples here are offered as historical markers so we can learn from their successes and failures. We have grouped them into four different models-----the single emperor model, the colonial model, the faith-based model, and the sovereign state association model.

Our current movement towards global citizenship and world community stands in contrast to the four models in our historical survey. This new movement represents a bottom-up model. It is not based on the charisma of a single ruler; on the dominance of a self-perpetuating dynasty. It is not obsessed with government structures and legal codes; but rather with building communities in different parts of the world whose members share common values. It is grounded in the increasing reality of peoples' globalized lives and their awareness that part of their identify has a global dimension to it. Its' governance institutions are emerging organically, in fits and starts, in response to the real needs that people have for standards and systems that can effectively support the global dimensions in their lives.

- (A) THE SINGLE EMPEROR MODEL

The Emperor-Based Model focuses on a single political leader (usually male) to whom people pledge allegiance, and who uses military force to gain control over ever larger amounts of territory. He usually is a person who sets out to conquer the world. The emperor/ leader is a charismatic person who promotes the adaptation of certain legal, social, economic, and cultural norms in which he believes. The emperor model usually ends when the emperor dies and is succeeded by a weaker leader, or when the emperor's armies are defeated by opposing forces.

- **The Macedonian Empire (800 BCE – 168 BCE)--**The Macedonian Empire arose during a period in history when rulers sought to demonstrate their greatness by expanding the amount of territory they controlled. It was the largest empire of its time stretching from the Adriatic Sea to the Indus River and beyond. The success of the Macedonian Empire was in large part due to the leadership of men like Alexander the Great and his father Phillip II, as well as strong military and governance systems. Its lasting legacy was its success in spreading the ideals and forms of Hellenic culture, including Greek thought, language, philosophy and governance methods.[102]

As ruler, Alexander the Great placed boundless focus on strong, organized and efficient government and financial systems. Citizens of the empire identified strongly with its cultural, linguistic and governmental systems. The Empire eventually extended its reach beyond what it could reasonably control. After the death of Alexander the Great, the strong control that he exercised over his Empire collapsed resulting in weak governance and civil war. Later, in the 2nd and 1st centuries BCE, due to weakened Macedonian institutions, and clashes with the Roman Empire, the Macedonian kingdom was dismantled and rule over much of its territory was taken over by the Roman Republic.[103]

- **Sassanid Empire (224 CE – 651 CE)** For nearly 400 years, the Sassanid Empire was considered to be one of the two main superpowers in Western Asia and Europe (the other being the Roman Empire). From approximately 224 to 651 CE, the empire expanded through present day Afghanistan, Iraq, Syria, Iran, Armenia, Georgia, Azerbaijan, Dagestan, Central Asia, Turkey, the Persian Gulf, Pakistan, and even some parts of India. The Empire was established by Ardashir I and was organized around a centralized government led by a robust and glorified monarch. Society was divided into four groups including priests, warriors, secretariats and commoners. This strict caste system outlived the Sassanid Empire and remained throughout the early Islamic period. By glorifying the monarch and establishing a strict social hierarchical system, citizens of the empire were able to strongly identify with their role in society and with the power that joined them together. Due to invasions of the Arab Caliphate, during the reign of Yazdegard III, the Sassanid Empire was demolished and rule over its territories was subsumed by Islamic powers.[104]

- *The Roman Empire (44 BCE - 476 CE)* The Roman Empire extended a culture and way of life associated with the city-state of Rome to large areas within Europe and the surrounding Mediterranean. From the beginning, the Roman Empire was heavily focused on territorial expansion and, at its zenith, its rule extended over 6.5 million km of land. It had great influence on the development of language, architecture, law, philosophy and religion throughout its territories. All citizens of the Empire were required to pay taxes and swear allegiance to the Emperor. In the late third century CE the Empire began dividing governance responsibilities between four emperors. As a result, in 476 power struggles ensued, and the Empire eventually collapsed.[105]

- **_Qing Dynasty of China (1644-1911)_** Historians often refer to the period of the Quing Dynasty as Imperial China. The Qing Dynasty, also known as the Manchu Dynasty, was able to conquer and govern the largest territory that China has ever covered. Growing bigger than present day China, territorial expansion was seen as key in order to gain power and authority. The Manchu Clan provided emperors who ruled the Quing Dynasty. The Manchuse were an ethnic minority that chose to promote mainstream Chinese culture and values. They supported Confucian thinking, art, and paternalistic governance.

The Qing Dynasty is well known for beginning the Great Wall of China, which was later augmented and enhanced during the Ming Dynasty. The other major contributions of the Qing include the concept of a centralized government, the unification of the legal code, development of the written language, and the currency of China. Through pledging allegiance to the emperor and the entirety of China, the population of the region was able to identify itself to the same common entity despite their territorial, cultural, and socioeconomic differences. In the late 19th century, the Qing Dynasty began to collapse due largely to internal conflicts, and the growing influence of Western powers on Chinese governance.[106]

- ***Napoleonic Empire (1804-1814/15)*** Upon establishing himself as Emperor of France in 1804, Napoleon Bonaparte set out to conquer the rest of Europe. Through years of military victories, known as the Napoleonic Wars, French culture, ideology and influence spread throughout the region and France became the definitive European power in the mid 19th century. At its peak, the Empire covered 44 million subjects, whose affairs were guided by the provisions of a Napoleonic legal code. The code promoted equality of treatment for the Empire's citizens and the establishment of citizen jury systems. Though citizens of the Empire still clung to their national and cultural identities, many began to glorify French norms, culture and perspectives. Following defeats by Spain and Russia in 1812, Napoleon lost power and his empire fell into disarray. Though Napoleon gained power for only a short period of time, the influence of his rule extended long after his passing.[107]

- **The Third Reich (1933--1945)** The ruling Nazi Party of 1930s-1940s Germany sought the ultimate establishment of a world government under German rule. Adolf Hitler, the German leader, espoused the belief that world peace could only be acquired "when one power, the racially best one, had attained uncontested supremacy." Hitlerdevised an ideological system of self-perpetuating territorial expansionism, which soon brought Germany into World War II against an alliance of European and North American countries. During the war, Germany conquered or controlled most of Europe and Northern Africa. The Nazis persecuted and killed millions of Jews, Romani people, and others as part of what they called the Holocaust Final Solution. Hitler's Empire, known as the Third Reich, collapsed with Germany's defeat by the Allied Powers in World War II in May, 1945.[108]

- **(B) THE COLONIAL MODEL**

Colonialism is the establishment, maintenance, acquisition and expansion of colonies in one territory by people from another territory. The term colonialism normally refers to a period of history from the late 15th to the 20th century when European nation states established colonies on other continents. The colonial model of governance usually originates from the needs of the colonizing country to expand trade and gain control over greater economic resources to support its burgeoning population. Often an element of paternalism is part of colonial ideology, as the colonizing country seeks to bring civilized behavior to the lands it conquers. The colonizing country establishes colonies, replicates its system of governance in the conquered territories, but considers its colonial subjects to be second-class citizens. The downfall of colonial models occurs when they become over-extended and cannot adequately exercise control over their territories; when they meet defeat by rival colonial powers; or when their citizens, moved by anti-colonial ideologies of self-determination, successfully rebel.

- **British Empire (1583-1783)** At the turn of the sixteenth century, the United Kingdom began to establish colonies, dominions, and mandates overseas as a means to enhance its wealth and spread its rule and influence throughout the world. The British Empire was the first and, to this date, perhaps only global empire in history, with fourteen territories on all continents. By the beginning of the 20th century, the Empire had brought together approximately one-quarter of the world's population and covered thirteen million square miles; approximately one-fourth of the world's land area. The British Empire promoted political, linguistic, social and intellectual frameworks that helped spread the values of Western civilization throughout the world.

Despite its success, the Empire could not sustain itself. In the face of a world-wide movement for territorial independence and self-determination the British Empire was forced to cede power to many of the territories that it ruled. However, it created a network of affiliated countries and territories, the British Commonwealth of nations, that to this day provides an associational identity for those peoples who were former British subjects. Countries that belong to the British Commonwealth promote democracy, human rights, rule of law, liberty, free trade, peace, and good governance.[109]

- **The Spanish Empire (1402-1713)** During the 15th century, Spain organized itself around a dual but unified monarchy involving the King of Castil and the King of Arragon. Though each ruled separate parts of Spain, the two Kings worked together to form joint domestic and foreign policies, and provided support for Spain's massive territorial expansion. The Western Hemisphere was the focus of this expansion, starting with Christopher Columbus' discovery of the American continent in the fifteenth century. Spanish colonies spread throughout the Americas and to the East as well reaching current day Guam and the Philippines.

The Empire spread Catholicism, the Spanish language and western ideals throughout its territories. Through religion and language in particular, the Spanish Empire was able to establish power and grow its economy as a result of territorial expansion. In the seventeenth century, Spain's power began to decline. Historians believe that the Battle of Rocoi in 1643 ended Spanish supremacy in Europe. In the twentieth century, during a worldwide decolonization movement, the Spanish Empire decreased significantly. As a result, today Spain only has power over the Canary Islands, Ceuta, and Melilla.[110]

- **Soviet Union (1922-1991)** The Union of Socialists Republics (USSR), or Soviet Union, gained its power through the forced spread of Communist ideology. Using a Communist-run, single-party political system, the Empire was able to unite nearly fifteen different states with a centralized, planned economy and cultural system . People saw themselves as citizens of the USSR and not necessarily citizens of their own countries. Cultural identities became rooted in the socialist nature of the Empire and previous national identities weakened greatly. Even today, nearly twenty years following the fall of the Empire, soviet cultural and linguistic traditions remain prominent in newly independent former-soviet states.

Though the Soviet Union was not ruled by an emperor and declared itself anti-imperialist, critics argue that it exhibited certain tendencies common to historic empires. Most scholars hold that the Soviet Union was a hybrid entity containing elements common to both multinational empires and modernizing nation states. It has also been argued that the USSR practiced colonialism. Supporters of the Soviet Union, meanwhile, reject such claims and argue that the relationship between the Soviet Union and its satellites was one of voluntary cooperation.[111]

- **The American Empire**   The United States has never sought to establish and maintain overseas colonizes. However, it has had the tag of "empire" placed upon it largely because of its military power, its economic wealth, and the values it espouses. "American Century is a term used to describe the United States dominance of much of the twentieth century in political, economic, and cultural terms. The United States influence grew throughout the twentieth century, but became especially dominant after the end of World War II, when only two superpowers remained, the United States and the Soviet Union. After the dissolution of the Soviet Union in 1991, the United States remained the world's only superpower, and became what some have termed a hyper power. Within the US, both liberals and conservatives promoted the idea of American exceptionalism, which helped underwrite the notion of America as an imperial power.[112]

With the new millennium there has been a growing consensus among historians and statesmen and women, that America's dominant role in world affairs (and thus its imperial status) is rapidly coming to an end. For example, the U.S. National Intelligence Council admitted for the first time in 2005 that America's global power was indeed on a declining trajectory. The Council noted that "the transfer of global wealth and economic power now underway from West to East are without precedent in modern history. This transfer was viewed as the primary factor in the decline of the United States' relative strength-even in the military realm. Under current projections, the U.S. will find itself in second place behind China in economic output by 2026, and behind India by 2050. An opinion poll in August 2010 found that 65% of Americans believed that their "country was now in a state of decline."[113]

- **(C) THE FAITH-BASED MODEL**

The faith-based model is based on the motivation of religious followers to integrate church and state and conquer other lands and convert subject populations to their system of belief. Those who promote this model usually do so in the belief that their religion is superior to others, and that followers of other religions are somehow inferior. They believe that a conversion to their faith is in the best interest of everyone, and seek to set-up a world that is unified by religion, where there are no church-state separations. Faith-based models usually falter when there are clashes between religious leadership and the secular political and military forces that are needed to implement this approach; or when the forces of other faiths prove too much to overcome.

It should be noted that many religions conduct multi-faceted efforts in order to convert people to their faith. Such efforts include missionary work, political persuasion, and even armed force (e.g. the crusades). However, efforts to spread religion are not necessarily the same as efforts to use religion as the basis for political empires; and efforts to establish an official state religion (where the practice of other faiths is tolerated) are not the same as efforts to establish a theocracy. As described below, Islam is the main example of a religion that has been used as the basis for a multi-state theocracy. However, Islam, as well as other religions have been recognized as the official religion in specific countries, such as Islam in Pakistan, Buddhism in Thailand and Judaism in Israel.

112

With the collapse of the Mongol administration of Islamic lands in the fourteenth and fifteenth centuries, a trio of Islamic Empires began forming across Asia: the Ottoman Empire in Asia Minor, the Safavid Empire in Persia, and the Mughal Empire in India. These three Empires were the result of centuries of Islamic state building and expansion, and at their height, they covered nearly the entire Islamic world. The only Islamic regions left outside their domain were West Africa and Southeast Asia. These three Empires also were significant because they provided the bridge between the medieval and modern periods of Islamic history.

The Ottoman Empire formed in the early 14th century and reached its peak by 1600.The Empire, ruled by an Ottoman Turk Suni dynasty, at its height extended from Turkey to Tunisia. It had a decentralized system of governance, leaving many of the lands it conquered with some abilities to rule themselves. The Ottomans were famous for their contributions to the arts, Islamic architecture, and technology. They fell into a gradual decline as a result of both internal disorganization and pressure from its external foes in Europe and Asia. Nevertheless, the Ottoman Empire survived through the First World War, and it was disbanded only in 1918. Out of the core of the Empire, in Asia Minor, came the present-day country of Turkey.[114]

The Safavid Empire originated in the early 1500s and was based in what is now known as Iran. The Safavids ruled territory across the Caucasus and into Western Asia, and established themselves as the largest Persian Empire of all time. They established Persia as an economic power between east and west. They ruled through a governmental system based on checks and balances between administrative units, and were know for their patronage of the arts. The

Safavid Empire differed from the Ottoman and Mughal Empires because it was a Shi'a Empire, and religious differences led to much antagonism between the Safavids and their Sunni neighbors. The Safavid Empire was the shortest-lived of the three post Mongol period Islamic Empires, suffering its final collapse at the hands of the invading Afghans in 1722. It forever influenced Persian nationalism, however, and out of the remnants of the Safavid Empire grew the present-day country of Iran.[115]

The Mughal Empire , was ruled by a dynasty of strong Persian leaders starting with Akbar the Great. At its height the Empire covered 115,000,000 people and most of the Indian sub-continent. The Mughals combined a strong central government that connected the different regions of their Empire with respect for basic human rights. Theirs was not so much a theocracy as they allowed the practice of Hinduism, Buddhism and other minority religions. They were a Sunni and Sufi-based Muslim minority who ruled over a Hindu majority population. However, they allowed Hindus to rise to senior positions in government and the military. The Mughals also made strong contributions to the art, architecture, and literature of their times. Like the Ottoman and Safavid Empires, however, the Mughal Empire's power eventually declined, and the Empire's territory was ultimately absorbed by the expansion of the British Empire in India in the mid-19th century.[116]

- **(D) The Association of Sovereign Nations Model**

The association of sovereign nations model represents an attempt by nation states to cooperate with one another to address global issues they cannot solve by themselves. It preserves an approach to power and authority that recognizes the supremacy of the sovereign state, while implicitly recognizing its limits in a globalized world. The model also supports individual

values, such as basic human rights, that can be claimed by people throughout the world as their

own. As such the Association of Sovereign States Model is a stepping-stone to a new age of

global citizenship, world community and participatory global governance described in this

book.

- **The League of Nations** *(1920 to1935)* Following WWI, the League of Nations, an

  intergovernmental organization, was established to combat the outbreak of future wars

  through collective security. The League sought to promote disarmament and the

  resolution of international disputes through negotiation. U.S. President Woodrow Wilson

  played a leading role in the formation of the League. In his famous Fourteen Points for

  Peace speech, Wilson highlighted the creation of the League as a means to avoid the

  future of another World War, and sought to gain support for the U.S. entry into the

  League among the American people. Although Wilson won a Noble Peace Prize for his

  work, the U.S. never joined the League. At its peak the League of Nations had 58 member

  states. It was the first institution that recognized the need for an international

  organization that could help sovereign states deal with issues that were beyond their

  borders and required collaboration. Due to a variety of structural weaknesses, the

  League was dismantled following World War II and was replaced with a seemingly more

  efficient and effective system known as the United Nations.[117]

- **United Nations (UN) (1945- present)** Following World War II, the victorious Allied

  powers established the United Nations to promote international peace and cooperation and solve the international economic, social and humanitarian problems that plagued the post World War II world. With the aims of being more effective than the League of Nations, the U.N. has grown to address many of today's global issues and works to develop and implement global economic and social development standards and policies, such as the Universal Declaration of Human Rights. It also has suffered at times from bureaucratic excess and administrative mismanagement, and has been the object of numerous internal and external efforts to remake it as a more efficient organization.[118] (See Chapter 8 for a more detailed description of the United Nations).

Chapter 12. REINVENTING HISTORY

From a global citizenship perspective, history can be seen as a series of efforts to develop communities to help people find identity and meaning in life. The first human communities were simple clan-like groups established to meet the hunter/gatherer needs of early humans living on the plains of East Africa.

Over time, as our early African ancestors emigrated to different parts of the world, the nature of human communities became more diverse. A variety of cosmologies, cultures and ways of being emerged to respond to environmental conditions that people faced in different parts of the planet. This trend towards decentralization continued for many thousands of years as divergent communities were constructed across the planet; communities based on geography, ethnicity, social affiliation and religious belief.

The growing number of diverse communities tended to reinforce the perception that people were different from one another, rather than part of a common species. Such perceptual differences contributed to frequent outbreaks of civil and ethnic strife, colonial conquests, two world wars, and countless other armed conflicts.

The communities humans formed also had to grapple with organizational issues about how political power and authority was exercised, commerce organized , wealth distributed, security managed, and relationships structured between governors and the governed and church and state. Communities also had to find ways to deal with the demands of their citizens for basic human rights. These demands grew over time as prosperity increased, security improved and new ideas about human freedom took root.

The way in which such organizational issues were addressed varied from community to community. History has left us with a large repository of lessons learned about our experience with the organization of human communities. Such lessons can assist with our current challenge of developing global community. Global citizens need to respect and learn from the diversity of cultures, faiths, and world views that have contributed to our history; while also recognizing and valuing the universality of human nature and inter-dependence of our human experience.

We have come full circle. The human race originated as a group of family-based clans that needed to develop values and ways of working together in order to survive in what was then the known world. Today we come together again against the backdrop of a much larger known world . We have the opportunity to draw upon 400,000 years of community building history, and select those elements of our experience that are worth carrying forward.

The task of building global community is not an easy one. Highly charged and complex problems must be addressed; such as the sheer numbers of people in world (estimated to surpass seven billion in the next several years); the dream that this many people have of achieving decent standard of living; the realization that our planet has a finite set of resources; the growing gap between rich and poor; the different ways in which countries are governed; the ability of authoritarian political regimes to seize control of weak nations and embark on programs of hostile territorial expansion; and the destructive power of weapons of mass destruction.

We now need to organize community-building conversations on a global scale, in as inclusive a way as possible, to define the values we share as citizens of the planet. How will our emerging global community resolve the value-laden tensions between promoting marketplace freedom and addressing the needs of those living in poverty; between principles of basic human rights and the practices of countries that flaunt them; between promoting religious pluralism and recognizing countries with state-sponsored religions; between economic growth and sustainable development; and between the need for security and existence of weapons of mass destruction. These are difficult issues to resolve, but the process we use for resolving them is almost as important as the nature of our solutions. Here are some brief background notes on each of these important issues, and suggestions about who needs to be involved in consensus-building conversations.

Between market freedom and social responsibility: In a global community, how much leeway should be given to the private sector to make deals and extract profits? What if market forces have a harmful impact on workers, poor people, women and children and other disempowered social groups? Should we support a social safety net that cushions the blows that occur as economic growth waxes and wanes? How can such a safety net be established and who would manage it?

Those that need to be involved in this conversation include leaders from multi-national companies, the global financial sector, the International Monetary Fund, World Bank, and World Trade Organization, ministers of commerce from both industrialized and developing countries, international and national labor unions, consumer organizations and non-governmental organizations working to address issues of poverty and basic human needs.

Between asserting and complying with basic human rights: The principle of respect for basic human rights has been enshrined for many decades in international agreements and treaties and needs to be established as a core value of our world community. However, a global conversation on human rights must find solutions for two types of human rights questions that to date have not been adequately addressed. On the one hand is the question of what can be done to effectively persuade countries that commit human rights violations to comply with international agreements and standards? On the other hand are questions related to the need to protect individual privacy in an age where technology encourages an almost unlimited free flow of all information. (The recent Wiki Leaks incident is an example of the tension between freedom of information and the need for some agreement on what constitutes an appropriate level of privacy.)

Those who need to be involved in this conversation include human rights activists, legal scholars and distinguished jurists, representatives from government regulatory agencies in different countries and the media industry.

Between religious freedom and state-sponsored religion: Religious pluralism also is a core principle of our world community. Because global citizens have the ability to live and work anywhere in the world, they also need to be able to worship as they please wherever they are. However there are still many countries where the ability of people to follow their own religious beliefs is limited or not allowed. An inclusive world community must find ways to build bridges of understanding between religions, and promote the practice of religious tolerance in those places where it is not being practiced.

A conversation about this issue should include religious leaders and practitioners from different faiths.

Between economic growth and sustainable development: Is it possible at the same time to increase the world's total productivity so that more people have access to a decent standard of living, care and feed for all of the planet's seven billion plus people, lessen the widening gap between the rich and poor, and find ways of sustaining the earth's limited natural resources? These apparently contradictory goals need to be reconciled through the coordination of policies and programs that deal with economic development, environmental protection, and poverty alleviation.

Those who need to be involved in this conversation include: producers and manufacturers from resource scarce industries, development planners from different countries, environmental economists, and environmental protection groups.

Between the need for security and the existence of weapons of mass destruction: The emerging global community needs to find more effective ways of managing security and restoring order in failed states. It needs to keep the world safe from the very real threat of terrorists and rogue political regimes, and guard against their coming into possession of weapons of mass destruction. We need to continue efforts to get rid of loose nuclear material limit the production of nuclear weapons and destroy existing stockpiles.

Those who need to be involved in this conversation include representatives from the United Nations, the International Atomic Energy Agency Association, military leaders, disarmament experts, citizens of failed states and war torn countries, and political journalists and media specialists.

Having global conversations in a productive way about these and other global issues will require a willingness to look at new paradigms of development and how the world is organized. It will require the ability to utilize principles and models from different political and economic camps, and the flexibility to change course if a recommended direction proves unworthy. It will require bringing together organizations and people who usually don't interact with one another; and having the patience to work through difficult issues in a way that enables everyone involved to have an ownership stake and faith in the outcomes.

New technologies and communications tools will facilitate our being able to have a productive dialogue about these issues. However, it is worth noting that technology can provide the infrastructure to enable us to have our conversation but cannot, in and of itself, solve our problems.

Those on the path to global citizenship have important roles to play as conveners of such discussions. We can assert the common human values that need to be the starting point for discussions about building world community. Such values include a commitment to basic human rights; the belief that our unity as a community draws strength from the diversity of our people and cultures, and that our earth and its resources constitute a precious environment that needs to be nurtured and sustained. Values such as these will serve as the touchstones for the challenging community-building conversations that need to take place.

PART IV: MOVING FORWARD

Chapter 13. SIGNPOSTS ALONG THE PATH

The path to global citizenship is not always clear, not always straightforward. Most of us currently have started our journey, and few of us have completed it. In some sense our destination is unknown. We all are embarked on a common project of trying to figure out what being a global citizen and living in a world community is like. Based on our experiences, we can point out to one another signposts along the path, many positive and encouraging, but some menacing and threatening. These are markers that are likely to either lighten our journey or trip us up. In Chapter 13 we provide some examples of these signposts, dividing them into *forces of light* and *forces of darkness.*

THE LIGHT FORCES: THE INTERNET, CELL PHONES, NGOs, GLOBAL ACTION NETWORKS, GLOBAL SOCIAL ENTREPRENEURS, ECUMENICAL COOPERATION, SPACE, THE ENVIRONMENT, EDUCATION, AND MEDIA REACH

- *The Internet:* The Internet is a powerful force helping to shape us into a global community. With its postal service, library, and social networking functions, the Internet lives up to its motto of being a "world-wide web." Currently there are an estimated 1.8 billion people who use the Internet, 28% of the world's 6.8 billion people.[119]

  The communications environment on the Internet is conducive to openness, transparency, and supporting the free-flow of information. These are enormously liberating factors in connecting people across the globe to one another. It often means that those living in information-restrictive societies have other ways of getting information and communicating with the outside world. In the past decade we have witnessed numerous instances where the Internet has been used to make the world aware of human rights abuses going on in different countries. For example in 2009, as a response to what many Iranians thought was a fraudulent presidential election, social networking sites such as Facebook and Twitter played a vital role in helping to organize popular protests and communicating what was going on in the country to the outside world. In Haiti and Chile in 2010, after devastating earthquakes had taken down local phone-lines, satellite supported internet access allowed local NGOs to provide news agencies and diaspora families with images of the extent of the devastation and to coordinate the provision of needed disaster relief supplies.[120]

There also is a dark side to the Internet. It is used to transmit information and propaganda by terrorists, drug dealers, pornographers, and other unsavory denizens of our planet. Some argue that communications on the Internet should be regulated. However, in looking at this issue, we also need to be mindful of attempts to regulate the Internet for purposes that are not so wholesome, i.e. the recent efforts by Egypt to close down the Internet so that democracy advocates could not use it as an organizing vehicle. *(For more on global citizenship and the use of social media, see Chapter 6.)*

- *Cell Phones:* The worldwide penetration of cell phones is another major force connecting people around the globe. Only eight countries in the world currently lack local cell phone providers (Nauru, Palau, Kiribati, Marshall Islands, Niue, Falkland Islands, Norfolk

Island, Western Sahara). Cell phones have become amazingly inexpensive and easy to

access. Trends in cell phone usage are on the uptick in every corner of the globe.

According to a UN Report published in 2009, six of every ten people in the world have

mobile telephone subscriptions. People from developing countries make up two-thirds

of all cell phone users.[121]

The growing number of inexpensive applications now enables cell phone users to do a

multitude of things without having to sit down at a computer. Now users are able to

connect with their peers, business partners, family and friends through email, chat, text

messaging, and video messaging directly through their mobile device. Additionally cell

phone users are able to download, edit, and send computer files, manage bank accounts,

check the weather, check the status of airplane flights, play games, read the news,

connect to social networks, take photos and send them immediately, manage their

calendars, download music, order subscriptions, get directions, view maps, and a

multitude of other things.

- *NGOs:* The growth of community-based and non-governmental organizations has been a

  powerful force for building global community. It is estimated that there are now over

  20,000 international NGOs, many of which are developing innovative ways for

  addressing world issues. This is not to say that all NGOs and community-based

  organizations (CBOs) have an affinity towards global citizenship. There are some, which

  are fronts for more parochial ideological and religious interests. However, large numbers of NGOs are helping people from around the world come together as global

citizens and address with global developmental and humanitarian issues of our time.

(For more on the role of NGOs in supporting global citizenship, see Chapter 6.)

- *Global Action Networks (GANs):* Steve Waddell has documented the evolution of GANS as

  part of an emerging global public policy system. GANs are formed by issue stakeholders

  joining together to develop solutions for a particular issue. Examples include the Global

  Reporting Initiative, Forest Stewardship Council, the World Commission on Dams,

  Transparency International, and the Marine Stewardship Council. GANs are formal

  organizations made up of groups of organizations ("members" or "participants")

  interacting with varying degrees of intensity and connectedness. GANs are global in

  scope, focused on action for the common good. Their members bridge traditional

  divides, such as sectoral (business-government-civil society), cultural and

  disciplinary.[122]

- *Global Social Entrepreneurs:* Global social entrepreneurs have come together to establish

  social venture funds that make investments in small and growing businesses (SGBs) and

  help improve the lives of people living in poor communities. With over $ 7 billion

  invested and 192 social venture funds established, these venture capitalists help bring

  change to the communities that need it most. In some developing countries, SGBs

  represent approximately 16% of the GDP. For every dollar invested in SGBs, another

$10 is generated in the local economy.[123] *(For more on how social entrepreneurs function as global citizens, see Chapter 6).*

- *Ecumenical Cooperation:* While the phenomena of fundamentalism garners many of today's headlines about religion, there also is a growing interest among spiritual leaders in inter-faith dialogue. The roots of ecumenical cooperation go back many centuries. In the 1500s the Emperor Akbar the Great encouraged tolerance among the Muslims, Hindus, Sikhs, and Christians living in Mughal India. Over the centuries leaders from all of the world's major religions have promoted tolerance and dialogue that can help affirm the common truths that all faiths promote. Today one finds the ecumenical tradition still very much alive. In 2000, Kofi Anan, U.N. Secretary General convened a Millennium World Peace Summit of religious and spiritual leaders. Those attending agreed to form a World Council of Religious Leaders to will help intervene in conflict areas of the world. The concept of respect for religious pluralism is a key value in the worldview of global citizens.

- *Space:* The idea of space exploration should serve as a unifying force for the peoples of the world. Space exploration offers us the possibility of unlocking the mystery of the universe, learning about external forces that affect our quality of life, and discovering new natural resources. These goals of space exploration are universal, and should motivate our leaders to work together to achieve them. It is difficult to organize space into territorial extensions of nation states or other provincially-minded domains; and so one would hope that exploration of space could be a journey that we collaboratively

take together.

The 1967 Outer Space Treaty acts as the basis of international space law. Over 98

countries are parties to the treaty, while another 27 have signed it but have not followed

through with steps for ratification. The treaty bars any parties from testing weapons in

space, conducting military action, establishing military bases, or installing WMDs in any

orbit of the Earth, Moon, or space body. Furthermore, the Treaty states that exploration

of space will be done to benefit all countries and that no State may claim sovereignty

over any outer space body.[124]

Despite the existence of the Outer Space Treaty, we must guard against space

exploration being a misguided extension of competition between nation states. For

example, countries with the ability to have their own space programs often seem to be

competition with each other to see who can be first to go to this or that planet. The costs

of serious space exploration are too great, and the resources available too few, to

organize our exploration of space in such a fragmented way.

- *The Environment:* Cleaning-up and protecting the quality of the earth's environment is an

  issue that almost everyone on the planet can support, no matter what your political or

  ideological persuasion. There are growing examples of citizens from different countries

  working together on environmental issues; for example the thousands of scientists from around the world who contribute to the important work of the Intergovernmental Panel on Climate Change, an institution established by the United Nations to monitor patterns of global warming. Global people-to-worldwide environmental issues such as climate change.[125]

- *Education*-- Schools, colleges, nonformal learning centers, and other educational institutions can play important roles in teaching the values, rights and responsibilities of global citizenship. Unfortunately, the prevailing educational paradigm in many countries focuses on *education for productivity*; as nations driven by the need to establish a competitive advantage for themselves seek to turn out skilled workers more productive than those of their economic competitors. There also are religious schools whose curriculum focuses on educating students to follow a fundamentalist way of life. However, many educators are developing curriculum frameworks that can be used by schools interested in following the path of global citizenship. Education for global citizenship provides students with access to opportunities to learn about basic human rights and the political, economic and social issues that face our planet. It offers teaching and learning activities to help students develop a more global perspective on life; for example by engaging in hands-on real world problem-solving activities with students from other countries *(For more on global citizenship education see Chapter 14)*

- *Media Reach:* The reach of radio, television and other forms of broadcast media also help people transcend the boundaries of their own cultures and worldviews. While a powerful argument can be made against the ethnic stereotyping and sex and violence that broadcast media often promote; this argument is offset by the ability of such media to convey important news, information and educational content to billions of people. Currently radio is still the predominant form of broadcast media in many parts of the world ; however access to television broadcast is increasing rapidly thanks to the growing number of satellite transmission and fiber optic networks and the electrification of most of the planet. The coming decade will witness the growing integration of broadcast media with the internet combining the use of television, computers, cell phones, SMS, and other rapidly emerging communications technologies.

THE DARK FORCES: RELIGIOUS FUNDAMENTALISTS, TERRORISTS, TRADE PROTECTIONISTS, ANTI-IMMIGRATIONISTS, SUPER PATRIOTS, TRIBALISM. BORDERS, AND MEDIA IMAGES.

- *Religious Fundamentalists:* Religious purists, who believe that literal interpretation of their faith or their founding scriptures is the only way in which life should be led, can be found in every religion. In Judaism religious fundamentalists are represented by groups such as Gush Emunim, Ateret Cohanim or Haredi Judaism; Islamic groups include the Wahabi tradition in Saudi Arabia, and the Taliban in Afghanistan; examples of Christian fundamentalist groups include the Westborough Baptist Church and the Independent Fundamental Churches in the United States. Most religious fundamentalists have a worldview that refuses to tolerate and barely recognizes the rights of other religions to exist. They do not accept a fundamental core principle of global citizenship, i.e. a respect for the practice of everyone to worship as they please.

132

Religious fundamentalists should not be confused with people living in countries that have a state religion, for example Thailand and Budhism, and Pakistan and Islam. Being a citizen of a state with an official religion does not preclude you from also being a global citizen. However, you might find yourself in conflict with your core principles if your state denied the ability of those not practicing the state religion, to worship as they please

- *Terrorists:* It goes without saying that terrorism is incompatible with global citizenship. The practice of extremist forms of politically or ideologically inspired violence only serves to make the world an insecure place in which to live, and reduces the climate for cooperation. However, terrorism sometimes can have a backlash effect of forcing the countries and people of the world to work more closely together to prevent terrorist attacks and collectively prosecute those who have committed such crimes.

- *Trade Protectionists:* The world also needs to guard against the practice of extreme economic protectionism, whereby countries enact high tariffs or engage in trade wars with one another. Such practices have the effect of shutting down trans- border commerce and the ability of people and businesses to work freely with one another.

- *Anti-Immigrationists:* Many countries are struggling with the issue of immigration, as large numbers of people cross their borders illegally. However the response to immigration concerns should not be to shut down borders completely and prohibit people who need to move (and who will find a way to move anyway) from doing so. That sort of anti-immigrationist stance mitigates against the ability of people to freely move across the planet, a principle of global citizenship. Global citizens need to press their countries to establish immigration policies that keep borders as open as possible, while in turn protecting the quality of life and rights of those already living there.

- *Super-patriots:* We still live in a world of nation-states, where many people take great pride in the accomplishments of their country. There is nothing wrong with that. However, those who believe that other countries are inferior to their own; who have no interest or concern in what goes on in the rest of the world are in denial of globalization and the inter-connectedness of people and their countries in the 21st century. The extent to which these super-patriots influence their country's political agenda often helps determine the ability of their governments to work collaboratively with other nations and solve issues that affect the world community.

- *Tribalism:* Tribal loyalties and ethnic allegiances are still a predominant form of political identify in many countries. In these nations such allegiances are a major force constraining the emergence of the practice of global citizenship. Can such countries leap-frog the nineteenth and twentieth centuries and become a part of our globalized age? Of course. Satellites, coaxial cables, and cell phones have made it possible for countries where tribalism is rampant to become globally connected. Young people, not as encumbered by traditional loyalties and digitally connected, can lead the way as they have recently shown us in Egypt, Tunisia, and other tribal bound countries of the Middle East.

- *Borders:* While much is made about the devaluing of traditional borders between countries, the fact is that they still exist; and they help to define who we are, who we become when we travel, and how the rest of the world views us ----"the American," the South African." Virtual global communities, international professional associations, multi-national businesses, and the experience of traveling to another country all help break down the influence that borders hold over us. Yet they are still there and will probably not go away anytime soon. What is becoming apparent is that people who need to ignore borders, for whatever reason, find a way to do.

- *Media Images:* The media have a tendency to promote inaccurate and incomplete images of life in different parts of the world. The image of the Middle East, for example, is of a place filled with terrorists waiting to abduct you or place a bomb in your bed. Africa is still often portrayed as a place filled with rampaging soldiers looting and pillaging every town in which they enter. Such images of course are a gross distortion of life as most people live it in the Middle East, Africa, and other media-hot locations. And yet media images often make other people feel cut off and afraid of these places and the people that live in them.

Chapter 14. STRATEGIES TO GET THERE

There is no master plan to make us all global citizens; nor should there be. Any movement to build a caring global community must take place organically, the product of the evolution of our attitudes and culture. A foundation stone of this book is that such a movement is currently taking place, fueled by the forces of modern communications, technology, and transportation. These forces in turn have spurred the development of global economic markets and social and professional networks, which in turn are going to require stronger governance mechanisms to develop equitable rules and promote cooperation between people and countries. The question is not whether or not we will have a global community but what kind of global community will we have? The answer to this question depends on a variety of factors within and outside of our control.

This chapter highlights such factors. We call them strategies to get there, and there are two types. The first type are big picture group strategies, i.e. those strategies which either affect large groups of people around the world or require broad based reform of existing political, economic, and socio-cultural systems. The second type are personal strategies that focus on transformations of attitude and behavior that individuals need to make in order to create a more caring human environment for the world in which we live.

Big Picture Strategies *include nurturing global leaders, organizing global citizen groups, reforming systems and institutions of global governance, strengthening the effectiveness of international law and treaties, protecting human rights, reducing the gap between rich and poor, protecting the environment; celebrating world heritage and cultural diversity, and promoting global citizenship education.*

- *Nurturing Global Leaders:* Perhaps the most important factor related to the development of a world community is the quality and skills of our global leaders - presidents and heads of state, global business executives, religious leaders, heads of civil society organizations and others. To what extent are our leaders willing to work together to develop policies and programs that support the well being of the planet as well as their own countries and institutions. We need leaders with the vision to see that the future well being of their own countries is inextricably linked to the future of the planet; the ability to engage their citizens in embracing the vision; and the courage to act on it.

- *Organizing global citizen groups:* We need global citizen groups to help build world community. Such groups would consist of people on the path to global citizenship interested in working with others on world community-building projects. Such projects can be on many different levels; for example projects that advocate taking a position on a global issue with governments and different international organizations; efforts to work with others on a humanitarian response to a disaster in a particular part of the world;

and activities that promote greater international exchange and dialogue among students, business people, artists. At the moment there are few institutions with the name global citizen group. There are, however, human rights groups, peace groups, environmental organizations and others which come close. Watch soon for the launch of a related website: www.globalcitizenassociation.org intended to support the organization of global citizen groups in different parts of the world.

- ***Reforming the systems and institutions of global governance:*** Many of the critical issues facing the planet are global in nature, dealing with poverty, health pandemics, the environment, trade and capital flows, energy and natural resource use . The political systems for addressing such global issues are a mixture of traditional sovereign states and emerging global governance institutions.[126] As discussed elsewhere (see Chapter 8) there is an urgent need to strengthen the management of these global governance institutions. They need to become more transparent, efficient, and directly accountable to the people whom they serve.

In addition there is a need for greater coordination among global governance institutions, which tend to operate in sector specific domains, e.g. health, agriculture, education. There is at the moment no locus of authority, agency or legitimacy to provide overall strategic guidance for defining the inter-institutional arrangements that are needed for the future. Leaders of global governance institutions are not empowered to make those kinds of strategic decisions. The U.N. Secretary General lacks the authority to undertake that level of strategic planning, and most national political leaders have little interest or time to address this issue in a serious manner.

- **STRENGTHENING THE EFFECTIVENESS OF INTERNATIONAL LAW AND TREATIES**

International law is the body of treaties and conventions that regulate the relationships between nations. The United Nations Treaties Series now includes over 50,000 international treaties covering topics ranging from taxation to torture. The international legal scholar Oona Hathaway argues that states now routinely make legal promises that are in direct conflict with the longstanding conception of state sovereignty, including delegating to international institutions authority that has traditionally been held solely by states. Hathaway argues that "With the ever-accelerating pace of globalization, international law is both more intrusive and more essential than it has ever been.[127] People, organizations, and governments are interacting with one another across borders more than ever before. These interactions lead to conflict that must be resolved, to cooperation that must be managed, and to confusion that must be clarified. Modern states cannot afford to reject international law or the tool of international delegation."

- **PROTECTING HUMAN RIGHTS**

The term "human rights" refers to basic rights and freedoms that all humans should be guaranteed, such as the right to life and liberty, freedom of thought and expression, and equality before the law. Modern international conceptions of human rights can be traced to the aftermath of World War II and the formation of the United Nations. The United Nations Charter states that one of the purposes of the U.N. is to "promote and encourage respect for human rights and for fundamental freedoms for all without distinction as to race, sex, language, or religion. The rights espoused in the U.N. Charter have been codified in a series of international covenants, such as the Universal Declaration of Human Rights, the International Covenant on Civil and Political Rights and the International Covenant on Economic, Social, and Cultural Rights.

While these agreements and covenants indicate near universal respect for the principles of human rights, much work needs to be done to ensure compliance. To date, it is assumed that the major responsibility for enforcing human rights rests with nation states; i.e. that it is the responsibility of each state to protect human rights within its own borders.

But, what if a state fails to live up to its obligations to enforce the principles of human rights? What are the avenues of appeal for someone, such as the recent Chinese Nobel Peace Prize winner Liu Xiaobo, who feels that they have been wrongly accused of human rights violations by their country? Or what if a country commits human rights violations outside its borders. The United States is arguing that its imprisonment in Guantanamo Bay without trial of foreign terrorists captured in Afghanistan and elsewhere does not constitute a human rights violation because they have been jailed outside the territorial confines of the US. As Professor Mark Giney argues: "The point is that human rights are universal, but so are the duties and responsibilities to meet those rights.[128] This is what the framers of all the human rights treaties sought to achieve. If human rights protection were something that individual states could (and would) do individually, there would be no need for any international conventions.

Stripped to their barest essentials, what each of these treaties represents is nothing less than this: that everyone has an ethical as well as a legal obligation to protect the human rights of all other people."

Global citizens can play important watchdog roles in relation to human rights compliance. We can help monitor compliance with international treaties and conventions, report human rights abuses in our countries, and monitor the treatment of those accused or imprisoned for human rights violations. There are a number of outstanding NGOs who work in this area, deserving of our support and participation.

- **REDUCING THE GAP BETWEEN RICH AND POOR COUNTRIES**

Today, approximately 20% of the world's population, at least one billion people, live on less than $1.00 per day. Half of the world's population lives on less than $2.50 a day. 80% of the world's population lives on less than $10.00 a day and more than 80% live in countries where income differentials between rich and poor are widening. The poorest 40% of the world's population accounts for 5% of total global income; while the richest 20% accounts for three-quarters of total global income.[129]

In the year 2000, under the auspices of the United Nations, leaders from 189 countries agreed on a set of Millennium Development Goals (MDGs) to be achieved by the year 2015. The MDGs were envisioned as a set of concrete, numeric benchmarks for tackling extreme poverty in its many dimensions. They include:

- halving the proportion of people whose income is less than $1 a day
- achieving full and productive employment and decent work for all, including women and young people
- ensuring that children everywhere, boys and girls alike, will be able to complete a full course of primary schooling
- eliminating gender disparity in all levels of education
- reducing by two-thirds the under-five mortality rate
- reducing by three-quarters the maternal mortality rate
- achieving universal access to reproductive health
- halting and reversing the spread of HIV/AIDS
- achieving universal access to treatment for HIV/AIDs for all those who need it
- halting and reversing the incidence of malaria and other major diseases
- integrating the principles of sustainable development into country policies and programs and reversing the loss of environmental resources
- achieving a significant reduction in the rate of biodiversity loss
- halving the proportion of people without sustainable access to safe drinking water and basic sanitation
- achieving a significant improvement in the lives of at least 100 million slum dwellers.

The MDGs represent a compact to alleviate poverty between all the world's major economic stakeholders. Poorer countries pledge to improve governance and increase accountability to their own citizens; wealthy countries pledge to provide the resources. Entire governments are committed to their achievement including the trade and finance ministers who hold the world's purse strings.

Performance against the goals is being monitored. Such monitoring takes the form of national Millennium Goal Reports, and Secretary General reports to the General Assembly. Those on the path to global citizenship have an opportunity to participate in MDG monitoring activities being carried out by civil society organizations in many countries.[130]

Above and beyond achieving the MDGs, reducing poverty also needs continued worldwide sustainable economic growth, which in turn requires good governance, prudent macroeconomic management, competitive markets and a vibrant private sector, efficient institutions and sustainable use of natural resources. It also requires reforms to reduce inequalities in human resource capabilities and access to assets and productive resources such as land, training, and credit.

- **PROTECTING THE ENVIRONMENT**

The environment is reflective of the global interconnectedness of our planet. All major environmental issues---pollution, climate change, biodiversity, and natural resource preservation----are global in nature. Over the past several decades' knowledge has increased about the causes of environmental problems and how to address them. A range of public policy options now exist for addressing environmental issues, including market-based instruments, public information programs, emissions standards, natural resource management policies and recycling and waste management policy.

Caring for the well being of our planet should be a core value of our emerging world community. We should advocate for sustainable development, i.e. development that meets the

144

needs of the present without compromising the ability of future generations to meet their own needs . However, we also must realize that with population growth and more and more people wanting a better standard of living, pressures on the world's ecosystems will increase unless there is a marked shift in human attitude and action.

Those on the path to global citizenship can help nurture the planet's environment in many ways, for example by making lifestyle changes that help reduce our carbon footprint, reducing consumption of threatened ecosystem services, buying products that are sustainably harvested, helping to monitor pollution levels in our communities, and advocating for changes in local, national, or international **environmental policies**

- *Celebrating world heritage and its cultural diversity* Unesco has an ongoing program of designating historical and cultural places around the world as "world heritage sites." Examples of such sites include the Great Barrier Reef in Australia, Brasilia, the capital of Brazil, the Great Wall of China, and Mount Kenya National Park. The World Heritage Site Program needs to be more widely publicized and expanded to include people and events, as well as places,that have contributed to world heritage. For example such designations could be given to famous artists and writers from different cultures, leading scientists and inventors, and those who are known for their worldwide humanitarian relief efforts. In this way awareness would be raised about the contributions of global citizens in different parts of the world that have helped unite us as a world community.

- ***Promoting global citizenship education*** Global citizenship education is used to help youth develop a deeper understanding of what it means to be part of a world community. It requires an approach to education that is focused on giving students the skills and experience needed to live and work productively with people from other cultures and engage in global problem solving. *(See Chapter 15 below for a more in-depth description of global citizenship education.)*

<u>PERSONAL STRATEGIES</u> *Personal strategies refer to individual actions that can be taken to help build world community by different types of people who are on the path to global citizenship. Here are some examples:*

- ***If you are a religious leader you may want to lead your congregation in speaking out against intolerance towards other religions; or speak out against members of your own religion who use your faith to justify intolerance towards those from other countries***

In 2010, Gainesville, Florida preacher, Terry Jones, announced his congregation's plans to burn thousands of copies of the Muslim holy book, the Koran on September 11th, a day he labeled "International Burn a Koran Day." Jones, head of the Dove World Outreach Center, a fundamentalist Christian Church, perpetually preaches anti-Islamic sermons to his congregation and associates global Islam with "the devil."[131] Jones' announcement sparked reactions and protests in countries around the world. In response to the announcement of Jones' actions, Reverend Andrew Heyes, of St. Clement Episcopal Church in Tampa, Florida, preached to his congregation against such action, as he believed it did not represent true

Christian values. Heyes stated: "It shows a lack of [the] Christian concept of grace and love that we should offer to all people, no matter of what faith or no faith." Though Jones' group is a small, fundamentalist group, Heyes believed that it was crucial to reassert the concepts of acceptance and tolerance by speaking out against what he believed was unjust and threatening to the loving nature of Christianity.[132]

Regrettably, despite the fact that religious leaders such as Heyes, spoke out against the burning of the Koran, Terry Jones decided to do it anyway. Given our global connectedness, and the immediacy of internet based communications, religious mullahs in Afghanistan immediately learned of Jones' book burning through the announcement of it on his congregation's website. They immediatelyset out on a lethal rampage that resulted in the deaths of foreigners living in Afghanistan.

- ***If you are an economist you may want to advocate for economic policies and programs that are win-win for the entire world and not just for a specific country.***

Ngaire Woods, Professor of International Political Economy and Director of the Global Economic Governance Program at Oxford University and advisor to the IMF Board and the UNDP's Human Development Report, openly argues against the continued liberalization of free trade as it currently stands. She believes that free trade produces positive and efficient outcomes for all parties only when conditions exist that allow **for** pure competition – something currently impossible given the economic discrepancies between developing and developed countries. Currently free trade benefits developed countries that have greater ability, resources, and monopolies for competition. Woods wants the World Trade Organization to make a greater effort to negotiate agreements and rules among its member countries countries that will increase trade efficiency and fairness.[133]

- *If you a business leader you may want to work with leaders of similar businesses from other countries and help develop global standards of fair practice*

Marissa Feinberg, former leader at General Electric, always felt passionately about dedicating herself to bettering the lives of people around the world. After leaving General Electric, she focused her efforts on connecting socially responsible business initiatives in different countries. Her passion and hard work resulted in her co-founding and acting as executive director of Green Leaders Global, a professional network that aims to unite business leaders around the world in setting standards for environmentally sustainable business practices. The network currently has more than 5,000 members.[134]

- *If you have more money then you need, you could join with other wealthy people and pledge to give away some of your fortune to help those in need in other parts of the world*

After retiring from the position of Senior Vice President of Programs at the Kellogg Foundation, philanthropist Anne Peterson decided to pursue her interest in global philanthropy and social entrepreneurship. In 2006, she connected with three other individuals from different countries who had similar interests, means, and goals. Together they created the Global Philanthropy

Alliance that works to link other philanthropists to help support youth-focused and youth-engaged NGOs developing countries.[135]

Another example of global citizen-based philanthropy is the "Giving Pledge," an effort led by Warren Buffet and Bill Gates to get the wealthiest families in America to give the majority of their wealth to charitable programs. So far 49 of America's most wealthy people have agreed to the "Giving Pledge;" and now Buffet and Gates are trying to convince wealthy people in countries like China and Great Britain to make the pledge as well.

- *If you are a musician you may integrate sounds and instruments from other cultures to enrich the music you make*

"Nowadays, nobody grows up doing just one thing. It may be perceived that music is on different floors, but it's all one house, and I have the choice to move from one room to another," says world famous cellist Yo-Yo Ma

Ma, perhaps the most well known figure in all of classical music, launched his Silk Road Project in 1998 in an effort to explore new ways of educating through art. The name alludes to an ancient trading route spanning thousands of miles and linking southern Europe to Africa, Asia and much of the Middle and Far East." I don't feel like I created something so much as organized a group of fellow interested citizens," Ma says.

The Silk Road Project commissions new music from composers around the world with the goal of stressing intercultural connections and the musical thread between then and now. Ma and fellow musicians perform these compositions in Silk Road concerts. "If you go deeply enough," Ma said, "you get to the world. You find how it spread all across the globe and you get a composite picture of what our planet's about and how we want to relate to each other."[136]

As for the actual concerts, there's no such thing as a "typical" program, Ma said. If there were, though, it might include traditional and contemporary works from China, the Middle East, India and the Galicia region of Spain. Ma plays cello, naturally, while others play Indian drums, Galician bagpipes, Chinese lute and a Japanese bamboo flute.

"People have stories, and they really want to tell them through music," Ma says. "It's just about what you feel is worthwhile. It's the same process that's been going on for thousands of years."[137]

- *If you are a teacher you want to establish a global classroom environment for your students*

While working in an urban public school in New Mexico, Danielle Figara realized quickly that she had to instill a global culture in her classroom. Her students came from a variety of cultural, religious and ethnic backgrounds. After viewing the conflicts and tensions between the various ethnic groups in her class, Danielle sought to sway her students' attention to their similarities rather than their differences. Every two weeks she established a thematic cultural topic where students spent time delving into a particular country's culture, history, difficulties, music, food, location in the world, religion, and worked on social justice projects. Danielle established a global culture in her classroom, which resulted in not only in increased cultural awareness, but also in decreased tensions among her students.

- ***If you are a farmer you may want to connect with farmers in other countries who are producing crops similar to yours and are interested in adapting sustainable agricultural practice***

For nearly four generations, Rodrigo Alvarez' family farmed the same plot of land in central Uruguay. Rodrigo and his family struggled to keep up with the technological innovations sweeping the farming industry. In an effort to learn more about ways of increasing productivity, he joined the International Federation of Agricultural Producers (IFAP). The IFAP, acts as the voice for the international farming community. With representatives from over 112 national organizations in eighty-seven nations, it facilitates communication and networking between farmers in both developing and developed countries. Farmers from different countries are able to share ideas and experiences. Quickly, through IFAP, Rodrigo joined forces with other Uruguayan and South American farmers to discuss common concerns. He learned of new ways to enhance his farm's technology and gained access to a large network of farmers who faced the same challenge – to farm sustainably while still being able to support themselves and their families. With the support of IFAP and the farmers he met, Alvarez was able to learn how he could adapt new sustainable framing methods and boost his farm's productivity.[138]

- ***If you are a fisherman you may want to advocate for industry practices that protect the type of fish you catch from being over-harvested***

Douglas Finno's family has been fishing off the waters of Alaska for hundreds of generations. Owning a small boat, Finno and his family caught little, yet enough to feed their families and sell to their community. Starting in the year 2000, the Alaskan seafood industry grew in size and importance. Finno's family could not compete and soon they realized that the large fisheries were threatening the livelihoods of local fishermen and the sustainability of fishing in Alaskan waters. Finno organized his fellow fishermen to meet with the leaders from the North Pacific Fishery Management Council (NPFMC). In the meeting Finno and his fellow fishing boat captain expressed sadness about the threat that large fisheries posed to their communities. The NPFMC responded by establishing more effective regulations to promote sustainable Alaskan fishing practices. Since then, the catch for small fishing boats in Alaska has begun to increase. Finno monitors the implementation of the NPFMC regulations and reports changes he witnesses to members of the Council.[139]

- ***If you are a student you may want to deepen your knowledge and understanding by studying your subject through the lens of another culture.***

Growing up in Shanghai, Shiu-Shiu Lee had a strong interest in politics and the practice of conflict resolution. She attended Shanghai University to study these subjects. In 2009, after a meeting her university counselor, Shiu-Shiu decided that she wanted to travel abroad to further her course of study. She had a fascination with Israel and the multitude of groups that resided there. Despite her parents' lack of approval, Shiu-Shiu decided to spend a year studying conflict resolution in Haifa, Israel. Upon arrival, she quickly realized she was one of only a few Asian students. She lived in a university apartment with Israeli and Arab roommates, learned Hebrew, and studied with Israel's top conflict-resolution professors. There she delved into the political, religious and cultural problems that grounded the conflicts within Israel. Her

approach to conflict resolution, as well as her understanding and perspective on life changed as

a result of studying in another country.

Chapter 15. EDUCATION FOR GLOBAL CITIZENSHIP

The prevailing logic of educational policy asserts that governments must improve human capital (especially in scientific fields), since only highly skilled individuals will thrive when pitted against competitors from across the planet for scarce jobs. Psychologically, the discourse of global competition stems from a view that students are entering an arena in which citizens of each country are pitted against each other for economic survival.

An example of this thinking can be found in Thomas Friedman's book, the *World Is Flat,* in which Friedman explains how his advice as a parent has changed. Rather than telling his daughters to be grateful for their food because children in India and China are starving, he tells his daughters to do their homework, because other children in China and India are starving for jobs.

Such a narrow focus on global competition in labor markets can displace broader dialogue about other purposes of education, particularly the purpose of preparing students to engage in activities that prepare them for the challenges of global citizenship, e.g. finding collaborative solutions to the many cross-national problems that vex our planet.

Education for global citizenship needs to take place across the curriculum. The incidental learning about global issues that young people may gain in traditional class lessons or through media can be helpful, but is insufficient to develop the full range of attitudes, knowledge, and skills associated with global citizenship. Educators should consider the many ways in which they can intentionally integrate a comprehensive approach to global citizenship throughout the K-20 spectrum of schooling. This approach should be grounded in the following knowledge domains:

- The theory and practice of basic human rights;
- The philosophies and sciences of ecological interdependence and sustainable development;
- The principles and practices of globalization and global economics;
- The belief systems that underlie the world's different religious and spiritual traditions, cultures, and political ideologies; and
- The theory and practice of international relations, peace-building, and global governance.

The knowledge domains noted above are intended to orient students to "think globally" in relation to economics, politics, ecology, and constructive social change; and help how to use these domains to better understand the multi-dimensional nature of global issues.

Today's students also need to develop an expanded awareness of what's going on around them, locally , and understand the ways in which "global" and the "local" dimensions of reality intermingle. For example, students might study the issue of migrant workers in their communities in relation to global economics, human rights, and shifting cultural identities. In this way, students can begin to draw what Katz (2001) thinks of as "contour lines" that connect local experiences with the experiences of distant others in an emerging topography of a global world.

Education also needs to address the affective dimension of global citizenship. Students need to be exposed to the domains of world music and art, connect with their peers in other countries to learn more about their interests and concerns, and make contributions to international humanitarian relief efforts.

Global citizenship education develops instructional programs that enable learners to practice the values associated with global citizenship. Examples of such instructional programs and activities include:

- Community service activities done in collaboration with people from other cultures/countries;
- Case studies and problem-solving activities in the transformation of conflicts between countries and cultures;
- a dialogue among learners from different countries regarding the definition of a global citizen's perspective on a particular world issue;
- Competency in more than one language and development of cross-cultural communication skills
- Integrated, experiential inquiry of the place of humans within local, bioregional, and earth ecologies;

- Contributions of indigenous knowledge and values to the building of world community.

There are several model global citizenship curricula now available for educators to use. One model has been developed by Oxfam (2006), which features themes of social justice, diversity, globalization, environmental sustainability, peace and conflict. This curriculum includes a rich framework for participatory activities that engage students in thinking critically about global issues and their local implications. The Oxfam model also includes an audit tool that educators can use to assess the climate for global citizenship in their schools.

Global citizenship education models also are being developed at higher education institutions. For example at the University of Wales global citizenship education is incorporated and embedded throughout the formal and informal education systems. According to the University of Wales website, integrating the concepts of "sustainable development and global citizenship into all aspects of education in Wales is a key policy objective of the Welsh Assembly Government."

Another interesting model is the United World Colleges (UWC) moment, which seeks to make education a force to unite people, nations and cultures for peace and a sustainable future. UWC is a British based foundation that supports thirteen schools and colleges and national committees in more than 130 countries. UWB offers the International Baccalaureate Program, a pre-sixteen syllabus, as well as tertiary level courses. At most UWC schools and colleges an average of 70 different nationalities are represented, helping students explore and develop international understanding. Her Majesty Queen Noor of Jordan serves as President of UWC; Nelson Mandela serves as honorary president.[140][141]

A recent Oxfam publication summarized education for global citizenship in this way: It " encourages young people to care about the planet and to develop empathy with, and an active concern for, those with whom they share it"

CHAPTER 16 . CONCLUSION AND CALL TO ACTION

I hope this book has enabled you to see what it means to be a global citizen. If parts of your life are globalized, as most peoples' lives are, you have the choice of being helplessly tossed around by the waves of globalization or weighing in to affect things by seeing global citizenship as part of your identity.

Being a global citizen does not preclude you from also being a citizen of your country. Global citizens accept the fact that multiple loyalties and allegiances—to family, religion, country, culture, and the planet at-large—are a fact of life today. We seek to build a world community that honors and respects such multiple allegiances, and strive to create collaboration among countries and peoples of the world.

While people identifying themselves as global citizens may share certain core values (e.g. respect for basic human rights, religious pluralism, and protection of the environment) global citizenship needs to guard against becoming labeled an ideology or identified with any particular political movement that might be seen to be exclusionary. The practice of global citizenship should involve inclusive debates, discussions and collaborative explorations by people with diverse perspectives who are connected by a commitment to find solutions to the issues facing our planet

Developing a complex, globally oriented identity comes with challenges. For many it may be uncomfortable to move outside the traditional boundaries and narratives that anchor our identity "close to home." It may be hard to begin asking questions about how local problems, to be properly understood, must take into account issues in distant places ; and difficult to find solutions that work for everyone. But because our local reality is so intertwined with what goes on across the planet, those on the path to global citizenship must take a hard look at questions such as these.

Taking the path to global citizenship also should be a joyful, inquisitive journey. It is all about seeing ourselves in new ways, and joining with others, who may seem quite different, to find the values that unite us. There are other choices for advancing into the future, but none that offers the vision of our unity and the celebration of our diversity, in the way that the path to global citizenship does.

What is most needed at the moment are leaders who share the vision of global citizenship, and who are willing to work together to provide the necessary leadership to further the vision. Hence this book concludes with the following Call to Action.

A GLOBAL CITIZENSHIP CALL TO ACTION

A global citizen is someone who identifies with being part of an emerging world community, and whose actions contribute to building this community's values and practices.

As a result of the serious problems that face our planet, the limited ability of nation states to solve these problems by themselves, the lack of greater accountability by global governance organizations, there is an urgent need to form an Initiative that can represent the values of the growing numbers of people across the planet who want to build global community. Such values include respect for basic human rights, the practice of religious pluralism, participatory governance, protection of the earth's environment, sustainable world-wide economic growth, poverty alleviation, humanitarian assistance, elimination of weapons of mass destruction, cessation and prevention of conflicts between countries, and preservation of cultural diversity.

This is a Call to Action for a member-based Global Citizens' Initiative that will help articulate and advocate for a global perspective to address world problems, promote the engagement of citizens in the growing number of organizations that contribute to global governance, and educate others regarding the values and responsibilities that come with global citizenship. More specifically, the functions of such an Initiative will include the following:

- **Advocacy:** The Initiative will advocate for approaches to solving world problems that best represent the interests of the global community as a whole. It will advocate for greater

161

citizen participation in efforts to address barriers to adopting global approaches to global problems that may exist at the local, national or international level.

- **Citizen Engagement:** The Initiative will build the capacity of its members to contribute to global governance policies and programs. It will identify and advocate for mechanisms that enable citizen groups to participate more fully in the decision-making process of global governance organizations.

- **Education:** The Initiative will support the development of instructional programs that educate and engage people in the practice of global citizenship. Such instructional programs will focus on the values and responsibilities of global citizenship, and be targeted to different audiences such as children, youth, professionals, and world leaders.

The Global Citizens' Initiative will establish a framework of civil discourse among its members. It will recognize that differences of opinion need to be sorted out and reconciled through honest dialogue and compromise. The Initiative will work closely with other institutions engaged in related activities. It will bring value added to the efforts of others, and seek their support for its own programs.

Those interested in joining such an Initiative are urged to register as members at The Global Citizens' Initiative.org. or contact: Ron Israel (RonCIsrael@yahoo.com).

End Notes

_____

[1] "How To Do Things » How To Articles & How To Videos." How To Do Things. http://www.howtodothings.com (accessed March 28, 2011).

[2] "Astronauts quotes? Help! - Topic." Quoteland.com User Groups. http://forum.quoteland.com/eve/forums/a/tpc/f/487195441/m/4731985985 (accessed March 29, 2011).

[3] "Olympic Games - Wikipedia, the free encyclopedia." Wikipedia, the free encyclopedia. http://en.wikipedia.org/wiki/Olympic_Games (accessed March 29, 2011).

[4] "Stock Market News & Financial Analysis - Seeking Alpha." Seeking Alpha. http://www.seekingalpha.com (accessed March 29, 2011).

[5] " IBLS." Internet Business Law Services. http://www.ibls.com/ (accessed March 29, 2011).

[6] Lewin, Tamar. "International Program Catches On in U.S. Schools - NYTimes.com." The New York Times. http://www.nytimes.com/2010/07/03/education/03baccalaureate.html?_r=1&ref=tam arlewin (accessed January 23, 2011).

[7] "Current Trends in U.S. Study Abroad and The Impact of Strategic Diversity Initiatives." Institute of International Education. Accessed March 21, 2011. http://www.iie.org/en/Research-and-Publications/Publications-and-Reports/IIE-Bookstore/Current-Trends-in-US-Study-Abroad-and-The-Impact-of-Strategic-Diversity-Initiatives.

[8] "Student decision making study - Education UK Marketing - British Council." British Council. http://www.britishcouncil.org/eumd-information-student-decision-making.html (accessed March 29, 2011).

[9] "International Federation of Red Cross and Red Crescent Societies (IFRC)." International Federation of Red Cross and Red Crescent Societies (IFRC). http://IFRC.org (accessed January 31, 2011).

[10] "History - Save the Children." Official Site - Save the Children. http://www.savethechildren.org/site/c.8rKLIXMGIpI4E/b.6229507/k.C571/History.htm (accessed January 23, 2011).

[11] "Sponsor A Child." Official Site. http://www.savethechildren.org/site/c.8rKLIXMGIpI4E/b.6146367/k.8EA1/Sponsor_A_Child (accessed January 23, 2011).

[12] "Kiva - About Kiva." Kiva - Loans that change lives. http://www.kiva.org/about (accessed January 23, 2011).

[13] "Sponsor a Child." Sponsor a Child. http://www.worldvision.org/ (accessed January 31, 2011).

[14] "Charitable Gift Giving that Makes a Difference." Heifer International. http://www.heifer.org (accessed January 31, 2011).

[15] "Habitat for Humanity Int'l." Habitat for Humanity Int'l. http://www.habitat.org (accessed January 31, 2011).

[16] "Press Room | Facebook." Facebook. http://www.facebook.com/press/info.php?statistics (accessed January 23, 2011).

[17] Tauber, Mike, and Pamela Singh. "Mixed Race Americans Picture A 'Blended Nation': NPR." NPR: National Public Radio: News & Analysis, World, US, Music & Arts : NPR. http://www.npr.org/templates/story/story.php?storyId=120209980 (accessed January 23, 2011).

[18] "ICAO | About ICAO." ICAO | International Civil Aviation Organization. http://www.icao.int/icao/en/m_about.html (accessed January 23, 2011).

[19] "Welcome to the International Federation of Accountants." International Federation of Accountants. http://www.ifac.org (accessed January 31, 2011)

[20] "The International Association of Fire Chiefs." The International Association of Fire Chiefs. http://www.iafc.org (accessed January 31, 2011).

[21] "World Wide Web Consortium." Wikipedia, the free encyclopedia. http://en.wikipedia.org/wiki/World_Wide_Web_Consortium (accessed January 31, 2011).

[22] "Global Art Project - for Peace." Global Art Project. http://www.globalartproject.org (accessed January 23, 2011).

[23] "Million Masterpiece - The world's largest collaborative arts project and online drawing community." Million Masterpiece. http://millionmasterpiece.com (accessed January 23, 2011).

[24] "Find People. Make Music. Online. - Indaba Music." Indaba Music. http://www.indabamusic.com/#!/logged_out/about (accessed January 23, 2011).

[25] "Connecting the World Through Music." Playing For Change. http://playingforchange.com/ (accessed January 30, 2011).

[26] "Olympics Statistics and History." Sports-Reference.com. http://www.sports-reference.com/olympics/ (accessed January 23, 2011).

[27] Gorman, Bill. "2010 World Cup Final on ABC: Most-Watched Men's World Cup Game Ever." TVbytheNumbers.com. http://tvbythenumbers.zap2it.com/2010/07/12/2010-world-cup-final-on-abc-most-watched-men%E2%80%99s-world-cup-game-ever/56837 (accessed January 23, 2011).

[28] Semone, Peter. "21st Century Trends in International Tourism. http://tourism101.org/archives/6 (accessed January 31, 2011).

[29] "GDRC | The Global Development Research Center." GDRC. http://www.gdrc.org (accessed January 31, 2011).

[30] "Migration Boom." *BBC News - Home*. Web. 21 Mar. 2011.
http://news.bbc.co.uk/2/shared/spl/hi/world/04/migration/html/migration_boom.stm.
[31] Bear, Michael. "Statistics on Humanitarian Relief." Human Rights | Change.org.
http://humanrights.change.org/blog/view/statistics_on_humanitarian_relief (accessed January 23, 2011).
[32] "Human Development Reports (HDR) – United Nations Development Programme (UNDP)." United Nations Development Programme (UNDP). http://hdr.undp.org/en/ (accessed January 23, 2011).
[33] "International Migration Guide." OneWorld UK. http://uk.oneworld.net/guides/migration#Global_Trends (accessed January 23, 2011).
[34] "Migration Boom." *BBC News - Home*. Web. 21 Mar. 2011.
http://news.bbc.co.uk/2/shared/spl/hi/world/04/migration/html/migration_boom.stm.
[35] Friedman, Thomas L. *The World Is Flat: a Brief History of the Twenty-first Century*. New York: Farrar, Straus and Giroux, 2005.
[36] Schoen, John W. "How Long Will the World's Oil Last? - Business - Oil & Energy - Msnbc.com." Breaking News, Weather, Business, Health, Entertainment, Sports, Politics, Travel, Science, Technology, Local, US & World News - Msnbc.com. Accessed March 21, 2011. http://www.msnbc.msn.com/id/5945678/ns/business-oil_and_energy/.
[37] Vidal, John. "The End of Oil Is Closer than You Think | Science | The Guardian." Latest News, Comment and Reviews from the Guardian | Guardian.co.uk. April 21, 2005. Accessed March 21, 2011.
http://www.guardian.co.uk/science/2005/apr/21/oilandpetrol.news.
[38] "Water Resources." Wikipedia, the Free Encyclopedia. Accessed March 21, 2011. http://en.wikipedia.org/wiki/Water_resources.
[39] "Human Appropriation of the World's Fresh Water Supply." The Global Change Program at the University of Michigan. Accessed March 21, 2011. http://www.globalchange.umich.edu/globalchange2/current/lectures/freshwater_supply/freshwater.html
[40] Water Treatment and Purification - Lenntech. Accessed March 21, 2011. http://www.lenntech.com/.
[41] "Destruction of World Forest's Continues, but Slows." America - Engaging the World - America.gov. November 14, 2005. Accessed March 21, 2011. http://www.america.gov
/st/washfile-english/2005/November/20051114165425cmretrop0.3126032.html.
[42] "Deforestation." Wikipedia, the Free Encyclopedia. Accessed March 21, 2011. http://en.wikipedia.org/wiki/Deforestation
[43] "More Effort Needed to Save the World's Forests | Connect-Green." Connect Green | Eco Friendly, Green Living, Green Products. October 10, 2010. Accessed March 21, 2011. http://www.connect-green.com/more-effort-needed-to-save-the-worlds-forests/.
[44] Rosenthal, Elizabeth. "Rush to Use Crops as Fuel Raises Food Prices and Hunger Fears." *New York Times Online*, April 6, 2011, sec. Environment. http://www.nytimes.com/2011/04/07/science/earth/07cassava.html (accessed April 12, 2011)
[45] "Decline in Fish Stocks | World Resources Institute." World Resources Institute | Global Warming, Climate Change, Ecosystems, Sustainable Markets, Good Governance & the Environment. Accessed March 21, 2011. http://www.wri.org/publication/content/8385.
[46] "World's Fish Stocks May Vanish in 40 Years." Sydney Morning Herald - Business & World News Australia | Smh.com.au. Accessed March 21, 2011. http://www.smh.com.
au/environment/conservation/worlds-fish-stocks-may-vanish-in-40-years-20100518-vcb4.html.
[47] "Climate Change." US Environmental Protection Agency. http://www.epa.gov/climatechange/ (accessed January 23, 2011).
[48] "Climate Change." US Environmental Protection Agency. http://www.epa.gov/climatechange/ (accessed January 23, 2011).
[49] "Climate Change Threats and Impacts." The Nature Conservancy.
http://www.nature.org/ourinitiatives/urgentissues/climatechange/threatsimpacts/index.htm.
[50] "Climate Change 101: Understanding and Responding to Global Climate Change | Pew Center on Global Climate Change." Pew Center on Global Climate Change | Working Together ...Because Climate Change Is Serious Business. January 01, 2011. Accessed March 21, 2011. http://www.pewclimate.org/global-warming-basics/climate_change_101.
[51] "Economic Growth and Human Development | World Resources Institute." World Resources Institute | Global Warming, Climate Change, Ecosystems, Sustainable Markets, Good Governance & the Environment. Accessed March 21, 2011.
http://www.wri.org/publication/content/8372.
[52] "Economic Growth and Human Development | World Resources Institute." World Resources Institute | Global Warming, Climate Change, Ecosystems, Sustainable Markets, Good Governance & the Environment. Accessed March 21, 2011.
http://www.wri.org/publication/content/8372.
[53] "Economic Growth and Human Development | World Resources Institute." World Resources Institute | Global Warming, Climate Change, Ecosystems, Sustainable Markets, Good Governance & the Environment. Accessed March 21, 2011.
http://www.wri.org/publication/content/8372.
[54] 2009, February. "Global Financial Crisis — Global Issues." Global Issues : Social, Political, Economic and Environmental Issues That Affect Us All — Global Issues. Accessed March 21, 2011. http://www.globalissues.org/article/768/global-financial-crisis.
[55] "United Nations Economic and Social Council." February 8, 2010. Accessed March 21, 2011.
http://www.un.org/News/Press/docs/2010/soc4761.doc.
[56] Fred, Wehlin. "International Regimes for WMD Nonproliferation and Control." Lecture, International Organizations Class from Monterey Institute of International Studies, Monterey, October 1, 2010.
[57] Fred, Wehlin. "International Regimes for WMD Nonproliferation and Control." Lecture, International Organizations Class from Monterey Institute of International Studies, Monterey, October 1, 2010.

[58] Fred, Wehlin. "International Regimes for WMD Nonproliferation and Control." Lecture, International Organizations Class from Monterey Institute of International Studies, Monterey, October 1, 2010.

[59] "The Challenges of Restoring Governance in Crisis and Post-Conflict Countries" (paper presented at the 7th Global Forum on Reinventing Government through the United Nations Department of Economic and Social Affairs and United Nations Development Programm, Vienna, Austria, June 26-29, 2007).

[60] "WHO | WHO Report on Global Surveillance of Epidemic-prone Infectious Diseases." Accessed March 21, 2011. http://www.who.int/csr/resources/publications/introduction/en/index4.html.

[61] Sturges, Janette. "How to Control a Pandemic of Communicable Diseases | EHow.com." EHow | How To Do Just About Everything! | How To Videos & Articles | EHow.com. Accessed March 21, 2011. http://www.ehow.com/how_5637840_control-pandemic-communicable-diseases.html.

[62] "What Is a Social Entrepreneur?" Ashoka.org. Accessed March 21, 2011. http://www.ashoka.org/social_entrepreneur.

[63] "Jody Williams: Land Mines and Networks." America - Engaging the World - America.gov. http://www.america.gov/st/democracyhrenglish/2009/March/20090304102443ebyessedo0.6759455.html (accessed January 23, 2011)

[64] "Adam Sterling on The Interviewpoint pt 1." YouTube. http://www.youtube.com/watch?v=j8KNjpp_eag (accessed January 23, 2011).

[65] "Adam Sterling's classes at UCLA impacted him more than he could have imagined. - Departments - UCLA Magazine Online." UCLA Magazine Online. http://magazine.ucla.edu/depts/quicktakes/out_of_africa_darfur_genocide/ (accessed January 23, 2011).

[66] Peschmann, Marinka. "Warren Buffett Funds Obama's International Fuel Bank?" Marinka Peschmann. www.marinkapeschmann.com/2011/01/20/warren-buffett-funds-obama's-international-fuel-enriched-uranium-bank/ (accessed March 28, 2011).

[67] "United Nations Foundation." Wikipedia, the Free Encyclopedia. Accessed March 21, 2011. http://en.wikipedia.org/wiki/United_Nations_Foundation.

[68] United Nations Foundation. Accessed March 21, 2011. http://www.unfoundation.org/.

[69] "Free Trade Vs. Fair Trade." Global Envision | The Confluence of Global Markets and Poverty Alleviation. http://www.globalenvision.org/library/15/834 (accessed January 23, 2011).

[70] "Fair Trade Cooperative Stories." Global Exchange - Building People-to-People Ties. Accessed March 21, 2011. http://www.globalexchange.org/cocoa/cocoacooperatives.html.

[71] "Labelling." Welcome to Fishonline. Accessed March 21, 2011. http://www.fishonline.org/buying_eating/labelling.php.

[72] "Sweden Introduces Climate Labelling for Food | EurActiv." EurActiv | European Union Information Website (EU and Europe). Accessed March 21, 2011. http://www.euractiv.com/en/cap/sweden-introduces-climate-labelling-food-news-222080.

[73] International Security Council. "Global Governance 2025:At a Critical Juncture." Global Governance 2025:At a Critical Juncture. www.dni.gov/nic/PDF_2025/2025_Global_Governance.pdf (accessed January 2, 2011).

[74] Bradford, Colin. "Global Governance Reform for the 21st Century." Global Governance Reform for the 21st Century. www.oecd.org/dataoecd/14/62/34983436.pdf (accessed January 2, 2011).

[75] Brain, Marshall. "HowStuffWorks "How the United Nations Works"." HowStuffWorks. http://www.howstuffworks.com/united-nations.htm (accessed January 23, 2011).

[76] Lynch, Colum. "U.N. struggles to prove its relevance." Washington Post. http://www.washingtonpost.com/wp-dyn/content/article/2010/09/19/AR2010091904173.html?nav=emailpage (accessed January 23, 2011).

[77] Bilefsky, Dan. "Recent U.N. Actions Show Policy Shift, Analysts Say." *New York Times Online*, April 5, 2011, sec. Africa. http://www.nytimes.com/2011/04/06/world/africa/06nations.html (accessed April 12, 2011).

[78] "The Court | International Court of Justice." Accessed March 21, 2011. http://www.icjcij.org/court/index.php?p1=1&PHPSESSID=26f0db34f7b21e0f66b814d2b6ca607c.

[79] "International Criminal Court." Wikipedia, the free encyclopedia. http://en.wikipedia.org/wiki/International_Criminal_Court#cite_note-cases-15 (accessed January 23, 2011).

[80] "International Criminal Court." Wikipedia, the free encyclopedia. http://en.wikipedia.org/wiki/International_Criminal_Court#cite_note-cases-15 (accessed January 23, 2011).

[81] "About the IMF." IMF -- International Monetary Fund Home Page. Accessed March 21, 2011. http://www.imf.org/external/about.htm.

[82] "About Us." World Bank Group. http://web.worldbank.org/WBSITE/EXTERNAL/EXTABOUTUS/0,,pagePK:50004410~piPK:36602~theSitePK:29708,00.html (accessed January 23, 2011).

[83] "About Us." World Bank Group. http://web.worldbank.org/WBSITE/EXTERNAL/EXTABOUTUS/0,,pagePK:50004410~piPK:36602~theSitePK:29708,00.html (accessed January 23, 2011).

[84] "WTO | About the organization." World Trade Organization - Home page. http://www.wto.org/english/thewto_e/thewto_e.htm (accessed January 23, 2011).

[85] "About IAEA: About the IAEA." International Atomic Energy Agency (IAEA). Accessed March 21, 2011. http://www.iaea.org/About/.

[86] "Interpol - Criminal Organizations." INTERPOL. Accessed March 21, 2011. http://www.interpol.int/Public/OrganisedCrime/default.asp.

[87] "Interpol." Wikipedia, the Free Encyclopedia. Accessed March 21, 2011. http://en.wikipedia.org/wiki/Interpol.

[88] Kouri, Jim. "INTERPOL Working in U.S. to Locate Criminals - National Law Enforcement." Examiner.com. Accessed March 21, 2011. http://www.examiner.com/law-enforcement-in-national/interpol-working-u-s-to-locate-criminals.

[89] "World Government." Wikipedia, the Free Encyclopedia. Accessed March 21, 2011. http://en.wikipedia.org/wiki/World_government.

[90] "World Government." Wikipedia, the Free Encyclopedia. Accessed March 21, 2011. http://en.wikipedia.org/wiki/World_government.

[91] "European Commission - Citizenship." EUROPA - European Commission - Homepage. Accessed March 21, 2011. http://ec.europa.eu/citizenship/programme-actions/doc18_en.htm.

[92] "G8." Wikipedia, the Free Encyclopedia. Accessed March 21, 2011. http://en.wikipedia.org/wiki/G8.

[93] "G-20 Major Economies." Wikipedia, the Free Encyclopedia. Accessed March 21, 2011. http://en.wikipedia.org/wiki/G-20_major_economies.

[94] "G8." Wikipedia, the Free Encyclopedia. Accessed March 21, 2011. http://en.wikipedia.org/wiki/G8.

[95] Florini, Anne. "Business and Global Governance: The Growing Role of Corporate Codes of Conduct - Brookings Institution." Brookings - Quality. Independence. Impact. 2003. Accessed March 21, 2011. http://www.brookings.edu/articles/2003/spring_business_florini.aspx.

[96] Florini, Anne. "Business and Global Governance: The Growing Role of Corporate Codes of Conduct - Brookings Institution." Brookings - Quality. Independence. Impact. 2003. Accessed March 21, 2011. http://www.brookings.edu/articles/2003/spring_business_florini.aspx.

[97] "2008 Global Accountability Report." One World Trust. 2008. 2008 Global Accountability Report.

[98] Bradford, Colin. "Global Governance Reform for the 21st Century." Global Governance Reform for the 21st Century. www.oecd.org/dataoecd/14/62/34983436.pdf (accessed January 2, 2011).

[99] Freedomhouse.org: Home. Accessed March 21, 2011. http://www.freedomhouse.org/.

[100] Nanz, Patrizia and Jens Steffek "Participation and the Public Sphere" in Global Governance and Public Accountability by David Held and Mathias Koenig-Archibug, Blackwell Publishing, 2005.

[101] Ferguson, Niall. "Complexity and Collapse." Foreign Affairs. http://www.foreignaffairs.com/articles/65987/niall-ferguson/complexity-and-collapse (accessed March 29, 2011).

[102] "Macedonia (ancient Kingdom)." Wikipedia, the Free Encyclopedia. Accessed March 21, 2011. http://en.wikipedia.org/wiki/Macedonia_(ancient_kingdom).

[103] "Alexander the Great." Wikipedia, the Free Encyclopedia. Accessed March 21, 2011. http://en.wikipedia.org/wiki/Alexander_the_Great.

[104] "Sassanid Empire - Wikipedia, the free encyclopedia." Wikipedia, the free encyclopedia. http://en.wikipedia.org/wiki/Sassanid_Empire (accessed January 23, 2011).

[105] "Roman Empire - Wikipedia, the free encyclopedia." Wikipedia, the free encyclopedia. http://en.wikipedia.org/wiki/Roman_empire (accessed January 23, 2011).

[106] "Chinese History - Qing Dynasty (www.chinaknowledge.de)." www.chinaknowledge.de. http://www.chinaknowledge.de/History/Qing/qing.html (accessed January 23, 2011).

[107] "First French Empire - Wikipedia, the free encyclopedia." Wikipedia, the free encyclopedia. http://en.wikipedia.org/wiki/First_French_Empire#The_Fall (accessed January 23, 2011).

[108] "Nazi Germany." Wikipedia, the Free Encyclopedia. Accessed March 21, 2011. http://en.wikipedia.org/wiki/Nazi_Germany.

[109] "British Empire - Wikipedia, the free encyclopedia." Wikipedia, the free encyclopedia. http://en.wikipedia.org/wiki/British_empire (accessed January 23, 2011).

[110] "Spanish Empire - Wikipedia, the free encyclopedia." Wikipedia, the free encyclopedia. http://en.wikipedia.org/wiki/Spanish_empire (accessed January 23, 2011).

[111] "Soviet Empire." Wikipedia, the Free Encyclopedia. Accessed March 21, 2011. http://en.wikipedia.org/wiki/Soviet_Empire.

[112] "American Century." Wikipedia, the Free Encyclopedia. Accessed March 21, 2011. http://en.wikipedia.org/wiki/American_Century.

[113] McCoy, Alfred. "The Decline and Fall of the American Empire - CBS News." Breaking News Headlines: Business, Entertainment & World News - CBS News. December 6, 2010. Accessed March 21, 2011.

[114] "Ottoman Empire." Wikipedia, the Free Encyclopedia. Accessed March 21, 2011. http://en.wikipedia.org/wiki/Ottoman_Empire.

[115] "Safavid Dynasty." Wikipedia, the Free Encyclopedia. Accessed March 21, 2011. http://en.wikipedia.org/wiki/Safavid_dynasty.

[116] "Mughal Empire - Wikipedia, the free encyclopedia." Wikipedia, the free encyclopedia. http://en.wikipedia.org/wiki/Mughal_empire (accessed January 23, 2011).

[117] "League of Nations." History Learning Site. http://www.historylearningsite.co.uk/leagueofnations.htm (accessed January 23, 2011).

[118] "United Nations - Credo Reference Topic." Credo Reference Home. Accessed March 21, 2011. http://www.credoreference.com/topic/united_nations.

[119] "Internet World Stats - Usage and Population Statistics." Internet World Stats - Usage and Population Statistics. http://www.internetworldstats.com (accessed January 25, 2011).

[120] "Internet Plays Vital Role in Earthquake Relief: Social Media Helps Haiti and Chile's Quake Disaster Efforts." Suite101.com: Online Magazine and Writers' Network. http://www.suite101.com/content/internetplays-vital-role-in-earthquake-relief-a207520 (accessed January 25, 2011).

[121] Vogt, Heidi. "World's Poor Drive Growth in Global Cellphone Use." USATODAY.com. http://www.usatoday.com/tech/news/2009-03-02-un-digital_N.htm (accessed January 25, 2011).

[122] Waddell, Steve, and Verna Allee. "Global Action Networks and the Evolution of Global Public Policy Systems." www.vernaalle.com. www.vernaallee.com/value_networks/ICSTM_paper_short.pdf (accessed April 12, 2011).

[123] Bloom, Evan. "Social Impact Investing." Lecture, Social Impact Investing Workshop from Monterey Institute of International Studies, Monterey, November 19, 2010.

[124] "Outer Space Treaty." Wikipedia, the free encyclopedia. http://en.wikipedia.org/wiki/Outer_Space_Treaty (accessed January 25, 2011).

[125] "United Nations Conference on the Human Environment." Wikipedia, the free encyclopedia. http://en.wikipedia.org/wiki/United_Nations_Conference_on_the_Human_Environment (accessed January 25, 2011).

[126] "TED Fellows - Home." TED Fellows. http://tedfellows.posterous.com (accessed January 25, 2011).

[127] Hathaway, Oona. "Presidential Power over International Law: Restoring the Balance." *The Yale Law Journal* 119, no. 2 (2009). http://www.yalelawjournal.org/the-yale-law-journal/content-pages/presidential-power-over-international-law:-restoring-the-balance/ (accessed March 24, 2011).

[128] Gibney, Mark, and Sigrun Skogly. *Universal human rights and extraterritorial obligations* . Philadelphia, Pa.: University of Pennsylvania Press, 2010.

[129] Global Issues: Social, Political, Economic and Environmental Issues That Affect Us All — Global Issues. Accessed March 21, 2011. http://www.globalissues.org/.

[130] "Millennium Goals - UNDP | Home." UNDP | United Nations Development Programme. Accessed March 21, 2011. http://www.undp.org/mdg/.

[131] Goldman, Russell. "Who Is Terry Jones? Pastor Behind 'Burn a Koran Day.'" ABCNews. http://abcnews.go.com/US/terry-jones-pastor-burn-koran-day/story?id=11575665 (accessed January 25, 2011).

[132] "Pastor Terry Jones still plans to burn Quran, but Tampa reverend will protest." Tampa Bay Fl News | WTSP.com. http://www.wtsp.com/news/local/story.aspx?storyid=144829 (accessed January 25, 2011).

[133] The Economist. "Debate: Fair Trade." Economic Debates. www.economist.com/ debate/days/view/510 (accessed January 20, 2011).

[134] "Leaders - Green Leaders Global." Green Leaders Global. http://greenleadersglobal.squarespace.com/ (accessed January 25, 2011).

[135] "Global Philanthropy Alliance." Global Philanthropy Alliance. http://www.globalphilanthropyalliance.org/ (accessed January 25, 2011).

[136] The Silk Road Project. Accessed March 21, 2011. http://www.silkroadproject.org/.

[137] O'Connor, David. "Yo-Yo Ma Takes Silk Road on Exploration of World Music | Cleveland.com." Cleveland OH Local News, Breaking News, Sports & Weather - Cleveland.com. August 13, 2010. Accessed March 21, 2011. http://www.cleveland.com/musicdance/index.ssf/2010/08/post_74.html.

[138] "IFAP: About IFAP." IFAP. http://www.ifap.org/about-ifap/en/ (accessed January 25, 2011).

[139] Blackford, Mansel. "ORIGINS | A Tale of Two Fisheries: Fishing and Over-Fishing in American Waters." eHistory. http://ehistory.osu.edu/osu/origins/print.cfm?articleid=18 (accessed January 25, 2011).

[140] United World Colleges. Accessed March 21, 2011. http://www.uwc.org/.

CPSIA information can be obtained
at www.ICGtesting.com
Printed in the USA
LVHW061310220819
628587LV00015B/357/P